Bob Weih

Contested Issues
of Ecosystem Management

Contested Issues of Ecosystem Management has been co-published simultaneously as *Journal of Sustainable Forestry*, Volume 9, Numbers 1/2 1999.

The *Journal of Sustainable Forestry* Monographic "Separates"

Below is a list of "separates," which in serials librarianship means a special issue simultaneously published as a special journal issue or double-issue *and* as a "separate" hardbound monograph. (This is a format which we also call a "DocuSerial.")

"Separates" are published because specialized libraries or professionals may wish to purchase a specific thematic issue by itself in a format which can be separately cataloged and shelved, as opposed to purchasing the journal on an on-going basis. Faculty members may also more easily consider a "separate" for classroom adoption.

"Separates" are carefully classified separately with the major book jobbers so that the journal tie-in can be noted on new book order slips to avoid duplicate purchasing.

You may wish to visit Haworth's website at . . .

http://www.haworthpressinc.com

. . . to search our online catalog for complete tables of contents of these separates and related publications.

You may also call 1-800-HAWORTH (outside US/Canada: 607-722-5857), or Fax 1-800-895-0582 (outside US/Canada: 607-771-0012), or e-mail at:

getinfo@haworthpressinc.com

Contested Issues of Ecosystem Management, edited by Piermaria Corona and Boris Zeide (Vol. 9, No. 1/2, 1999). *Provides park rangers, forestry students and personnel with a unique discussion of the premise, goals, and concepts of ecosystem management. You will discover the need for you to maintain and enhance the quality of the environment on a global scale while meeting the current and future needs of an increasing human population. This unique book includes ways to tackle the fundamental causes of environmental degradation so you will be able to respond to the problem and not merely the symptoms.*

Protecting Watershed Areas: Case of the Panama Canal, edited by Mark S. Ashton, Jennifer L. O'Hara, and Robert D. Hauff (Vol. 8, No. 3/4, 1999). *"This book makes a valuable contribution to the literature on conservation and development in the neo-tropics. . . . These writings provide a fresh yet realistic account of the Panama landscape." (Raymond P. Guries, Professor of Forestry, Department of Forestry, University of Wisconsin at Madison, Wisconsin)*

Sustainable Forests: Global Challenges and Local Solutions, edited by O. Thomas Bouman and David G. Brand (Vol. 4, No. 3/4 & Vol. 5, No. 1/2, 1997). *"Presents visions and hopes and the challenges and frustrations in utilization of our forests to meet the economical and social needs of communities, without irreversibly damaging the renewal capacities of the world's forests." (Dvoralai Wulfsohn, PhD, PEng, Associate Professor, Department of Agricultural and Bioresource Engineering, University of Saskatchewan)*

Assessing Forest Ecosystem Health in the Inland West, edited by R. Neil Sampson and David L. Adams (Vol. 2, No. 1/2/3/4, 1994). *"A compendium of research findings on a variety of forest issues. Useful for both scientists and policymakers since it represents the combined knowledge of both." (Abstracts of Public Administration, Development, and Environment)*

Contested Issues of Ecosystem Management

Piermaria Corona
Boris Zeide
Editors

Contested Issues of Ecosystem Management has been co-published simultaneously as *Journal of Sustainable Forestry*, Volume 9, Numbers 1/2 1999.

Food Products Press
An Imprint of
The Haworth Press, Inc.
New York • London • Oxford

Published by

Food Products Press®, 10 Alice Street, Binghamton, NY 13904-1580

Food Products Press® is an imprint of The Haworth Press, Inc., 10 Alice Street, Binghamton, NY 13904-1580 USA.

Contested Issues of Ecosystem Management has been co-published simultaneously as *Journal of Sustainable Forestry,* Volume 9, Numbers 1/2 1999.

Cover design by Thomas J. Mayshock Jr.

Library of Congress Cataloging-in-Publication Data

Contested issues of ecosystem management / Piermaria Corona, Boris Zeide, editors.
     p. cm.
     "Has been co-published simultaneously as Journal of sustainable forestry, volume 9, numbers 1/2 1999."
     Includes bibliographical references.
     ISBN 1-56022-065-1 (alk. paper)–ISBN 1-56022-067-8 (pbk.: alk. paper)
     1. Ecosystem management. I. Corona, Piermaria. II. Zeide, Boris.

QH75.C6845 1999
333.75–dc21
                                                        99-051660

INDEXING & ABSTRACTING

Contributions to this publication are selectively indexed or abstracted in print, electronic, online, or CD-ROM version(s) of the reference tools and information services listed below. This list is current as of the copyright date of this publication. See the end of this section for additional notes.

- *Abstract Bulletin of the Institute of Paper Science and Technology*

- *Abstracts in Anthropology*

- *Abstracts on Rural Development in the Tropics (RURAL)*

- *AGRICOLA Database*

- *Biostatistica*

- *BUBL Information Service, an Internet-based Information Service for the UK higher education community, URL: http://bubl.ac.uk/*

- *CNPIEC Reference Guide: Chinese National Directory of Foreign Periodicals*

- *Engineering Information (PAGE ONE)*

- *Environment Abstracts*

- *Environmental Periodicals Bibliography (EPB)*

- *Forestry Abstracts; Forest Products Abstracts (CAB Abstracts)*

- *GEO Abstracts (GEO Abstracts/GEOBASE)*

- *Human Resources Abstracts (HRA)*

- *Journal of Planning Literature/Incorporating the CPL Bibliographics*

- *Referativnyi Zhurnal (Abstracts Journal of the All-Russian Institute of Scientific and Technical Information)*

- *Sage Public Administration Abstracts (SPAA)*

- *Sage Urban Studies Abstracts (SUSA)*

- *Wildlife Review*

(continued)

*Special Bibliographic Notes related to special journal issues
(separates) and indexing/abstracting:*

- indexing/abstracting services in this list will also cover material in any "separate" that is co-published simultaneously with Haworth's special thematic journal issue or DocuSerial. Indexing/abstracting usually covers material at the article/chapter level.

- monographic co-editions are intended for either non-subscribers or libraries which intend to purchase a second copy for their circulating collections.

- monographic co-editions are reported to all jobbers/wholesalers/approval plans. The source journal is listed as the "series" to assist the prevention of duplicate purchasing in the same manner utilized for books-in-series.

- to facilitate user/access services all indexing/abstracting services are encouraged to utilize the co-indexing entry note indicated at the bottom of the first page of each article/chapter/contribution.

- this is intended to assist a library user of any reference tool (whether print, electronic, online, or CD-ROM) to locate the monographic version if the library has purchased this version but not a subscription to the source journal.

- individual articles/chapters in any Haworth publication are also available through the Haworth Document Delivery Service (HDDS).

Contest Issues
of Ecosystem Management

CONTENTS

ABOUT THE EDITORS

Piermaria Corona, PhD, has been Associate Professor of Forest Inventory at the University of Florence, Italy, since 1992. He was Adjunct Professor of Sylviculture at the University of Basilicata, Italy, from 1986 to 1992, and Researcher at the Centro di Sperimentazione Agricola e Forestale of Rome, Italy, from 1985 to 1992. He has been a member of the Italian Academy of Forest Sciences, since 1998. He authored over 100 scientific publications, and a book, dealing with various aspects of forestry. His main research fields are forest multiresource inventory and monitoring, forest management planning, and environmental issues.

Boris Zeide, PhD, is Professor of Forestry at the University of Arkansas at Monticello. He is known for innovative approaches to modeling population dynamics of forest stands, discovery of two basic forms behind existing growth equations, research in fractal geometry of tree crowns, and detecting effects of environmental change on forest ecosystems. Dr. Zeide's current studies include a balanced analysis of biodiversity and examination of the conceptual basis of ecosystem management. He has held eight visiting positions in different countries and authored over 150 publications dealings with technical, ethical, and philosophical aspects of forestry.

Conceptual Issues
of Ecosystem Management

Boris Zeide

SUMMARY. This paper examines the premise, goals, and concepts of ecosystem management. Evidence and philosophy of traditional forestry do not support the premise that it (forestry) is environmentally destructive. The goals of ecosystem management–to maintain and enhance the quality of the environment on the global scale, and to meet current and future needs of an increasing human population–are highly desirable. It is doubtful, however, that they can be satisfied simultaneously. The absence of well-defined boundaries of ecosystems is another obstacle to their management. One of the primary objectives of ecosystem management is maintaining and increasing biodiversity. Besides technical problems, there is a conceptual difficulty: we still do not know what biodiversity is. Equating biodiversity with everything is enlightening, but not too helpful since it is not clear how to manage everything. Operationally both concepts (ecosystem and biodiversity) are meaningless. Even if we manage to define biodiversity and delineate ecosystems, it won't help much because ecosystem management is designed only to treat symptoms of environmental decline, rather than its cause. *[Article copies available for a fee from The Haworth Document Delivery Service: 1-800-342-9678. E-mail address: getinfo@haworthpressinc.com <Website: http://www.haworthpressinc.com>]*

Boris Zeide is Professor of Forestry at the School of Forest Resources, University of Arkansas, Monticello, AR 71656-3468 USA (E-mail: zeide@uamont.edu).

This paper does not necessarily reflect positions of the School of Forest Resources, University of Arkansas, or other organizations. The author thanks Piermaria Corona, Brian Lockhart, Julia Parker, and Mike Shelton for many useful comments and suggestions.

[Haworth co-indexing entry note]: "Conceptual Issues of Ecosystem Management." Zeide, Boris. Co-published simultaneously in *Journal of Sustainable Forestry* (Food Products Press, an imprint of The Haworth Press, Inc.) Vol. 9, No. 1/2, 1999, pp. 1-20; and: *Contested Issues of Ecosystem Management* (ed: Piermaria Corona, and Boris Zeide) Food Products Press, an imprint of The Haworth Press, Inc., 1999, pp. 1-20. Single or multiple copies of this article are available for a fee from The Haworth Document Delivery Service [1-800-342-9678, 9:00 a.m. - 5:00 p.m. (EST). E-mail address: getinfo@haworthpressinc.com].

KEYWORDS. Definition of biodiversity, ecosystems boundaries, environmental decline, goals of ecosystem management, symptoms vs. cause

INTRODUCTION

Forestry is in the process of a fundamental reevaluation of its philosophy and methods. There is a general consensus that ecosystem management is the way to manage ecosystems in general, and forests in particular, at times of continuing environmental deterioration. However, proclaiming ecosystem management as a "wave of the future" and enforcing it is not the best way to attain a sustainable environment. The definition of forestry as the science and art of managing forests probably covers ecosystem management as well. Even the development of science is no longer viewed as a straightforward advancement from ignorance and superstition to knowledge and rational beliefs. According to Kuhn's (1970) widely held position, most often science switches between fashionable "paradigms" without much tangible progress. Arts are even more notorious for their fads. Despite all of this, we are certain that the progress from "old" to "new" forestry is not an example of such debilitating somersaults. Examining the premise, goals, and concepts of ecosystem management may help to elucidate this certainty.

PREMISE:
"OLD" FORESTRY IS NOT SUSTAINABLE

Dale Robertson (1992), Chief of USDA Forest Service, declared on June 4, 1992, that ecosystem management is the "Forest Service way." Robertson's attempt to describe ecosystem management was vague and limited to a politically correct statement designed to please both industry and environmentalists: "we must blend the needs of people and environmental values in such a way that the National Forests and Grasslands represent diverse, healthy, productive and sustainable ecosystems."

Actually, the first two adjectives are redundant because they are implicit in the other two. Diseased and genetically impoverished forests can hardly be productive and sustainable. Sustainability implies health and diversity of useful organisms. Jack Ward Thomas, Robertson's successor, stressed sustainability as the main point of ecosystem management in his picturesque talk with American senators. They asked Thomas to "explain–in simple and straightforward terms–just what was the purpose of 'ecosystem management.' " I asked the senator, "Did your momma ever tell you the fable of the goose that laid the golden eggs?" The senator allowed that he had heard the story. I then inquired, "Do you remember the lesson of that fable?" The senator replied that the point of the story was that "if you want golden eggs, it would be well to take good care of the goose." "Bingo!" I replied. "Such is the purpose of ecosystem management" (Thomas 1997, p. xi).

Ecosystem management is considered to be a "paradigm shift of massive proportions" (Franklin 1997, p. 21). "Shift" from what? Apparently, away from "old" forestry. We have here two propositions: (1) Sustainability is the goal of ecosystem management; and (2) Ecosystem management is introduced to replace traditional forestry. This shift was intended not so much to correct minor problems as to achieve that goal. From these statements it logically follows that ecosystem managers view traditional forestry as not sustainable. It does not matter whether this premise of ecosystem management is written explicitly in the official documents of the Forest Service or not. This would be too offensive to our profession. What does matter is that this premise is built into the two propositions contained in any description of ecosystem management.

Cynics say that ecosystem management is just a new name for the old multiple use. By insisting that ecosystem management is something radically different from "old" forestry and that its goal is sustainability, the exponents of this new paradigm are forced to conclude (if they still accept the old-fashioned Aristotelian logic) that traditional forestry is unsustainable and thus environmentally detrimental. This premise is critical to ecosystem management. If "old" forestry was sustainable, ecosystem management would be unnecessary.

There is evidence that some forestry practices do hurt the environment. They include treeless slopes denuded after clearcuts, degraded status of coppice forests in the Mediterranean basin, decreased productivity of some intensive eucalyptus plantations in India, poor regeneration after clearcuts on fragile soils in moist tropical regions and waterlogged areas in northern Russia, polluted streams, and others. All this evidence, however, has nothing to do with professional forestry. The forester is the first to condemn such practices. Clearcutting on steep slopes is a poor logging practice, repeatedly decried by foresters. From many studies, we know the relationship between slope, stand density, harvesting methods, and erosion for various soils. Based on this knowledge, we are in a position to decide when a clearcut or a selection harvest is appropriate. We use the same scientific approach to other problems such as productivity of intensively managed plantations.

Foresters feel proud of their profession because of the overwhelming evidence of healthy and productive forests. Even more important than this evidence is the principle that has guided all of our activities since the inception of the forestry profession–the principle of sustainable management. This principle includes, but is not limited to, timber production. The Multiple-Use, Sustained-Yield Act of June 12, 1960, mandates that "Sustained yield of the several products and services means the achievement and maintenance in perpetuity of a high-level annual or regular periodic output of the various renewable resources of the National Forests without impairment of the productivity of the land" (Anonymous 1974). All we do is to satisfy the needs of society. We are after a sustainable flow of clean water, the production of berries and mushrooms, and pleasing vistas. We enjoy them no less than city dwellers–that is why we choose forestry as our profession. We take care of nesting cavities when society demands and to pay for them. When we supply the material to produce paper and construction lumber, it is again only because people demand it.

As do other managers, foresters have their share of mistakes. But as soon as it becomes clear that a given activity contradicts the chief principle of forestry, we stop practicing it, and do everything possible to correct the mistake. As a result of our activities, the land that society trusted to foresters (not loggers) is in good shape, unlike depleted fisheries, eroded agricultural fields, and the deteriorating planet in general.

Natural attraction to new developments works in favor of ecosystem management. It is often presented as a new environmental paradigm, natural evolution of forest management, and, of course, a "wave of the future." Professor Mendelsohn (1994) expressed well this aspect of ecosystem management: "Many foresters, steeped in the traditions of their personal training, may get the mistaken notion that forestry has remained constant over the centuries and that this urge for change is a challenge to everything that a professional forester ever stood for" (p. 1); "American forestry has always been changing. The forestry profession should recognize that change has always been part of its character and resilience" (p. 5). The problem here is that Mendelsohn has confused the main issue with secondary particulars. It is true that many technical aspects of forestry have changed. But the essence of forestry, the principle of sustainable management, has not.

When proponents of "new" forestry address evidence, it becomes difficult to demonstrate that "old" forestry decreases forest productivity and endangers sustainability. A good example is a recent collection of 16 studies on ecosystem management published by Yale University Press and prefaced by Jack Ward Thomas (Boyce and Haney 1997). The collection portrays ecosystem management as "an idea whose time has come" (Thomas 1997, page xi), and says that "our future existence on this planet depends on [ecosystem management]" (Haney and Boyce 1997, p. 12), which is viewed as "millennial paradigm shift" (Franklin 1997, p. 21). Yet, the admissions made at the beginning reduce the force of the arguments in the rest of the book, if not refute them outright. Despite all the faults of "old" forestry, it does not cause environmental degradation: "Timber harvests of old growth, shifts in the relative abundance of cover types, fragmentation by roads or clearcuts, and even loss of some species would not appear to interfere with forest productivity. . . . Most forests in eastern United States were heavily exploited less than one hundred years ago. Much of the forest land that was cleared and used for agriculture now supports productive forests again. Although soils were badly eroded and species were lost, available evidence does not suggest that sustainability of second growth forests has been reduced. . . . Perhaps careful forest and wildlife management can be carried on in many areas indefinitely without ecosystem degradation or other severe consequences" (Haney and Boyce 1997, p. 2).

To conclude, the premise of ecosystem management that traditional forestry is unsustainable is not supported by evidence of and philosophy in forestry. Forestry has nothing to do with land abuse. It was, and is, about sustainable management of the land.

GOALS OF ECOSYSTEM MANAGEMENT

Unlike anthropocentric forestry of the past concerned only with man, ecosystem management, as Robertson's (1997) declaration shows, pursues two goals at once: (1) maintain and enhance the quality of the environment on a global scale, and (2) meet current and future needs of an increasing human population.

To achieve the first goal, environmental managers should set aside land to protect endangered species such as kangaroo rats and spotted owls, restore wetlands, provide an ecstatic experience of wilderness, and avoid destructive (that is, intensive) management of the remaining, productive parts of the landscape. "Natural resource managers must now learn how to manage natural communities, assemblages of species, indeed, the vast majority of wildlife" (Knight 1996, p. 472) rather than manipulate artificial monocultures. Ecosystem management is concerned with "maintenance and restoration of structurally diverse forests. . . . Techniques include use of a wider variety of tree species, provision for standing dead trees and down logs, and silvicultural treatments to create structural diversity. Partial cutting–retention of live and dead tree structures at time of harvest–is, in many areas, replacing traditional clear-cutting practices which effectively eliminated structural legacies that provide continuity from one disturbance to the next" (Christensen 1996, p. 674). The bottom line of these environmentally benign management practices is that the proportion of resources available for nonhuman beings should be increased.

The second goal acknowledges that, along with spiritual aspirations, humans have also material needs. With a possible exception of the Endangered Species Act, federal laws dealing with the environment consistently affirm the principle that natural resources are for the "use and enjoyment of the American people." This goal means that more and more resources have to be extracted from the shrinking productive land base to raise the standard of living for our growing population.

Since it has more than one goal, some view ecosystem management as a tough issue: it is not easy to decrease resource consumption to save the Earth and at the same time increase it to satisfy growing human needs and wants. More precisely, it is a conflicting issue. The difference is that tough issues can be resolved, conflicting–cannot. Until we stop our population and economic growth, environmental degradation and loss of biodiversity are inevitable. Each of the goals is highly desirable. However, since the Earth is finite, it is not feasible to attain both. Neither integrated holistic science, nor broad spatial and temporal scales, knowledge of complex interactions and linkages, monitorings and surveys could make the impossible possible.

CONCEPTS AND PHILOSOPHY
OF ECOSYSTEM MANAGEMENT

Sustainability of certain resources, be it timber, clean water, or berries, is only one of many objectives in ecosystem management. Unlike "old" forestry which is restricted to the land allotted by society for growing trees to benefit humans, ecosystem management is concerned with the global environment and all forms of life. Ecosystem management is not only wider but deeper than the outdated techniques of the bygone era. In addition to the technical disciplines that guided traditional forestry (dendrology, mensuration, cruising, economics), ecosystem management is based on a broader array of scientific disciplines which include ecology, sociology, esthetics, and history. Another indispensable component of ecosystem management is ethics or, more precisely, the expansion of ethics that covers not only human beings, but other living beings and landscapes as well. Ecosystem management not only benefits from existing science but also prompts and contributes to its development. Recently, we have witnessed the birth of new branches of knowledge such as conservation biology, restoration ecology, biodiversity studies, the subdiscipline of ecosystem health and integrity, land ethic, and environmental economics.

Although the all-embracing, scientific, creative, and unselfish nature of ecosystem management is irresistible, our duty is to examine its scientific foundation and determine whether this management system will be able to secure a clean and sustainable environment. With this in mind, we will consider the basic management questions: what, where, how, and why to manage.

Object of Management: Biodiversity

Maintaining and, better yet, maximizing biodiversity is one of the primary objectives of ecosystem management. The current attitude to biodiversity is expressed by its chief advocate Edward Wilson (1992, p. 32) of Harvard University: "every scrap of biological diversity is priceless, to be learned and cherished, and never to be surrendered without a struggle." This call may be too farfetched. After all, diseased organisms full of parasites and harmful bacteria are more biologically diverse than healthy ones. As compared with a stand of vigorous and healthy trees, one composed of diseased and decaying trees is more "biodiverse." And corpses have still greater biodiversity, if it is measured by the number of species. Are we really wanting to cherish all that biodiversity?

It is not easy to define this concept. Any definition pigeonholes and restricts the defined term. Biodiversity defies any restriction and may be indefinable in principle. Biodiversity encompasses the total abundance of organisms, species, populations, communities, and their environments together with all of their complex interrelations. Extraterrestrial factors such as sunlight cannot be excluded either. In short, biodiversity embraces everything. If so, we should not worry about biodiversity because, being everything, it cannot be lost. It could only change form. When one species disappears, others thrive. Equating biodiversity with everything is not a polemic exaggeration. Recently Wilson (1997, p. 1) himself acknowledged as much: "Biologists are inclined to agree that it [biodiversity] is, in one sense, everything." Knowing the one-sided nature of the biodiversity movement (its blindness to the detrimental side of biodiversity), it is entirely consistent that this "one sense" is the only one Wilson discusses.

The biodiversity movement is peculiar in lumping together species and individuals that–for us–are useful, harmful, and harmless. Yet, every one of us follows this basic taxonomy, whether realizing it or not. This division varies with time, place, and circumstance. Depending on the situation, we may reassign a certain species, but always into one of these classes. We will never have complete information about the utility of any species, yet we cannot postpone all action indefinitely. To exist, we must fight harmful species, consciously or unconsciously. This reaction is not restricted to humans. All creatures have to instantly classify species into the same three groups. A deer is afraid of humans and dogs; it is attracted to greenbriar vines and blueberry bushes; and it is indifferent to woodpeckers and caterpillars. This behavior is adaptive. A deer possessed by a love of all creatures or a grouse contemplating the inscrutability of species function would soon be torn up by coyotes, or killed first in a hunting season. The division of species as good and bad may be old-fashioned and narrow-minded, but without this concept nobody would be around to mind any fashion, old or new.

Locus of Management: Ecosystem

It is expected that ecosystem management is practiced within natural boundaries of ecosystems, rather than within artificial limits of old-fashioned forties, sections, or lines of private properties. However, unlike organisms, which always have specialized structures (bark, skin, etc.) that separate them abruptly from the environment, ecosystems do not have well-defined boundaries other than those produced by changes in the physical environment. Any ecologist is free to delineate an ecosystem at will. Surely, freedom in general is admirable, but the lack of identifiable boundaries turns ecosystem management into irreproducible science.

Ecosystem and Superorganism

The ecologist may find the concern about precise boundaries of a managed area exaggerated. The point is *how* rather than *where* to manage. What is important is to manage each piece of land, be it ecologically artificial private property or a natural watershed, according to ecological principles. And, the larger the piece, the better because of the intrinsic interconnectedness of all life on our planet and beyond.

The Forest Service defines ecosystem management as "the use of an ecological approach that blends social, physical, economic, and biological needs and values to assure productive, healthy ecosystems" (Kaufman et al. 1994, p. 16). Instead of wasting time on nitpicky arguments about boundaries, this definition is about larger issues. It catches the spirit of ecosystem management that should guide its applications and indicates that "an ecological approach" is something all-encompassing. Like biodiversity, it covers everything ("social, physical, economic, and biological needs and values"). Although it is not easy to specify these ecological principles or "an ecological approach," all of them are based on the notion of the unity and the holistic nature of our world. Perhaps, the tenet that "everything is connected with everything" grasps best the gist of those principles and approaches.

This essence is incarnated by the term "ecosystem," which was introduced by A.G. Tansley in 1935. At that time ecologists were focused on communities of plants and animals, which some of them considered as "superorganisms," "biotic communities," and "complex organisms." Aside from linguistic caveats (he preferred instead "quasi-organisms"), Tansley (1935, p. 290) had nothing against organism as an analogy of biotic communities. Actually, he was proud of his own contribution to this view, which "greatly strengthens" it: "the comparison with an organism is not merely a loose analogy but is firmly based, at least in the case of the more complex and highly integrated communities, on the close inter-relations of the parts of their structure, on their behaviour as wholes, and on a whole series of other characters which Clements ('16) was the first to point out. In 1926 (p. 679) I called attention to another important similarity which, it seems to me, greatly strengthens the comparison between plant community and organism–the remarkable correspondence between the species of a plant community and the genes of an organism, both aggregates owing their "phenotypic" expression to development in the presence of all the other members of the aggregate and within a certain range of environmental conditions."

It is commonly believed that the concept of ecosystem was proposed as an alternative to the problematic Clementsian "superorganism." Thus, Berlyn and Ashton (1998, p. 141) write that "The main purpose of Tansley's paper was to provide a dissent from, and an alternative to, the Clementsian dogma that a plant community is a 'superorganism.' " Similarly, Golley (1993, p. 201) believes that Tansley "formulated the ecosystem concept as an alternative to superorganisms and similar general categories." Yet, he acknowledges that "ecologists still confuse Clements's superorganism and ecosystems" (Golley 1993, p. 201).

The problem is that the first among these "confused" ecologists was Tansley himself. From his paper it clearly follows that he intended only to tie the "superorganism" to the land, to embed it into the environment: "the more fundamental conception is, as it seems to me, the whole *system* (in the sense of physics), including not only the organism-complex, but also the whole complex of physical factors forming what we call the environment of the biome–the habitat factors in the widest sense. . . . It is the systems so formed which, from the point of view of the ecologist, are the basic units of nature on the face of the earth. . . . These *ecosystems,* as we may call them, are of the most various kinds and sizes" (Tansley 1935, p. 299). Thus, an ecosystem is simply the "super" or "quasi" organism of biotic communities plus its environment. Figuratively speaking, an ecosystem is a superorganism on clay footing.

Tansley's concept is not a curious relic from the remote past. Besides corroborating details such as Lindeman's (1942) trophic-dynamic analysis, ecosystem stands now as it was defined by Tansley. Here is the definition of ecosystem from the most popular contemporary textbook of ecology: "A holistic concept of the plants, the animals habitually associated with them and all the physical and chemical components of the immediate environment or habitat which together form a recognizable self-contained entity. The concept is due to Tansley (1935)" (Begon et al. 1996, p. 958).

To an unprejudiced observer, the fallacy of the "super" or "quasi" organismic view is obvious. What we call an ecosystem is the opposite of an organism: it is an environment of plants and animals. Unlike an organism, this ambience is not something whole. If half of a forest stand is converted into a parking lot, the remaining half may occasionally lose an animal species, but usually is able to continue its existence as before, despite some possible changes in the hydrological cycle. Many ecologists believe that "loss of species could directly curtail the vital services that ecosystems provide to people" (Langhorst 1999, p. 69). This belief is debatable. While an organism disintegrates or becomes dysfunctional with the loss of a single limb or an enzyme, a field is not destroyed when not just one but all native plants and the animals depending on them are replaced by a single introduced species such as wheat in the Great Plains. The most productive forests in New Zealand, England, France, and other places are monocultures of introduced species. These examples are given here not to advocate monocultures. Sometimes mixed stands are more productive. The intention is to show that loss of species does not directly curtail the vital services that ecosystems provide to people. Moreover, in many cases this loss is the prerequisite for these vital services.

There are many other differences between organisms and biotic communities. Members of an organism die or survive together. In contrast, many components of what we call an ecosystem thrive at the expense of others. Each biotic part of an ecosystem, an organism, is much more complex than the ecosystem itself. The reverse is true for the organism. The theory of evolution and much of biology are based on the fact that the organism is the unit of natural selection; ecosystems are not. Examining the arrangement of plants in a forest stand "are we not justified in coming to the general conclusion, far removed from the prevailing opinion, that an association is not an organism, scarcely even a vegetational unit, but merely a coincidence?" (Gleason 1926, p. 16). This individualistic view of community is another extreme. Probably, the truth is somewhere in between the superorganism and individualistic views, though not in the middle. Considering community characteristics and their dynamics interrupted by disturbances, the truth appears to be closer to the individualistic end. The term "ecosystem" a misnomer. A system means a set of coordinated parts that form a whole, such as an animal body or an engine. The precision of a body differs in kind from what would be better called an eco-medley.

Looking at a perplexing assembly of plants and animals, their variegated interactions, accumulation of detritus and evolution of soil, succession of species, inevitable recovery from disturbances, and many other busy activities, it is tempting to consider an ecosystem unfathomedly complex. The authors of Boyce and Haney's (1997, pages x, 2, and 240) collection repeatedly cite or rephrase this sentence "Ecosystems are not only more complex than we think, but more complex than we can think." The impression of complexity often results from a lack of understanding, which can be produced by either of two causes. The insufficient knowledge of observed patterns or processes is one. Another is simply the absence of regular patterns or processes. We can't learn much when there is nothing to learn about. When these two reasons are confused, we may ascribe a profound complexity to a pile of stones. Or to perceive the patently chaotic Brownian movement as infinitely complex. It may be that, after all, ecosystems are more simple "than we can think."

It is curious that while the underlying concept of "superorganism" is largely discredited, "ecosystem" survives and even prospers, engendering vast practical applications in the form of ecosystem management. Still, the success of "ecosystem" does not add clarity to our understanding of the concept. At the same time, perhaps its very obscurity may be an asset for managing fittingly tangled forest ecosystems. Currently, ecologists argue whether ecosystems are conceptual or real physical entities (Cork 1998). Given the organismic fallacy, it would be more accurate to place them into the group of misconceptual entities. As for ecosystem management, it seems that its "how" (to manage assuming that ecosystem components are indispensable and interconnected like organism's parts) is no more sound than the considered "what" and "where."

Ethics and Ecosystem Management

Our difficulties with defining what, where, and how to manage ecosystems may be dismissed as niggling. Above these technical questions, there is the "why" of ecosystem management that makes the rest petty in comparison. For true believers, "ecosystem management is not defined. It is not a prescription; it is not even a process. It is simply a label for an attitude about resource management, one which widens and deepens our thinking about our actions. It is a component of the evolving land ethic" (Tarver 1995, p. 60). Such higher, ethical ground is doubly convenient: it serves to justify ecosystem management as well as to brush aside the evidence about beneficial results of forestry practices. This ground includes related teachings such as the land ethic, conservation ethics, environmental ethics, and biophilia. Presently these views are considered to be the basis of ecosystem management, making it morally superior to "old" forestry. All of these teachings reject the outmoded anthropocentrism and tend in various degrees to the opposite doctrine, known as eco- or biocentrism.

Ecocentrism is an appealing philosophy. It proclaims that all entities (including humans) should have the freedom to unfold in their own way, unhindered by human domination. Ecocentrism enhances and expands our most cherished values: unselfishness, justice, and equality. It picks up the torch of moral righteousness dropped with the collapse of communism. As Marxism did in the past, ecocentrism aspires to help the downtrodden and persecuted; this time nonhuman beings. It is symptomatic that ecosystem management was inaugurated the year after the fall of the Soviet Union. Ecocentrism opposes the view, called "speciesism," that one species is superior to others; the view which is similar to racism and is as outrageous. Regardless of what was written in ancient books, our exploitative domination over other species is unfair and unjust. Ecocentrism appears to be the next step in the evolution of ethics. This step outdoes in morality all the preceding ethical teachings of Western civilization. Unlike the previous advances, this one is infinitely large and final because ecocentric ethics embraces everybody and everything.

The question is whether this all-encompassing embrace leaves room for our existence. To answer it, consider two main propositions of ecocentrism: (1) all species have inherent value and various rights (such as well-being and flourishing) of which paramount is the right to exist; and (2) we, humans, are the only species capable of formulating and recognizing this right, and it is our obligation to respect it. With his customary eloquence Leopold presented this point well. When a monument to the Passenger Pigeon was dedicated in 1947, he wrote: "For one species to mourn the death of another is a new thing under the sun. . . . Had the funeral been ours, the pigeons would hardly have mourned us. In this fact, rather than in Mr. DuPont's nylons or Mr. Vannevar Bush's bombs, lies objective evidence of our superiority over the beasts" (Leopold 1966, p. 110).

The problem is that these two propositions contradict each other. To exercise our right to exist (the first proposition), we have to eat, which means to kill or exploit other species and organisms. These actions are prohibited to us by the second proposition. Without it, the abstract recognition of inherent values and the proclamation of rights are meaningless. To be consistent, the compassionate attitude Tarver (1995) talks about should include the suicidal respect of the right of other animals to kill us for food. However attractive ecocentrism may sound, it would be hazardous to build management on such a conflicting foundation.

Biophilia

In the process of inventing "moral reasoning of a new and more powerful kind" to cherish and protect life, Wilson (1984) coined a term "biophilia." He defined it as the inborn affinity human beings have for other forms of life. This feeling has far-reaching implications. The most important of them is that biophilia provides the foundation for "an enduring conservation ethic." "If a concern for the rest of life is part of human nature, if part of our culture flows from wild nature, then on that basis alone it is fundamentally wrong to extinguish other life forms. Nature is part of us, as we are part of Nature" (Wilson 1994, p. 362).

As are more conventional ethical teachings, Wilson's is supportive of such basics of human spirit as our perpetual expansion and personal freedom. (Since it requires personal freedom and results in perpetual expansion, producing children is doubly qualified as such basics.) On the other hand, as ecocentrism, this enduring conservation ethic is intended to save the environment from the same humans who produce too many children and want a higher and higher, that is, unsustainable standard of living.

Just as is biodiversity, biophilia is plagued from lumping together the incompatible things: harmful and useful species. Surely, we all are repelled by cruelty, and love kittens and puppies. But why forget our less charitable attitude toward parasitic worms and lice? Do we really feel any affinity or love for chiggers and mosquitoes? Species have played a contrasting role in our evolution. Some were useful, some were competitors and enemies, a threat to our survival. Accordingly, we have developed affinity and even love for the first group and abhorrence for the second. Natural selection would not trick us into liking harmful creatures. Our aversion to them helped us to survive. To cover both emotions by the same word "biophilia" (which means not affinity but love for living beings) is misleading. Love for other forms of life, biophilia, is not natural or unnatural. It is meaningless. We love some species and individuals and hate others. It is not our whim. We have been conditioned to do so: natural selection eliminated the inflexible whose capabilities were limited to one-sided responses. If the outside world were invariably benign, love would suffice and we would not be equipped with a spectrum of emotions.

Notions such as biophilia would not be worth discussing if they were shared only by a few eccentric personalities. Oddly, biophilia and similar views are widely held and inaugurated as the ruling philosophy of environmental management. For example, Stephen Gould (1991, p. 14), another renowned Harvard professor, wrote these stirring words: "we cannot win this battle to save species and environments without forging an emotional bond between ourselves and nature as well–for we will not fight to save what we do not love."

This sounds fine if Gould stopped there. Instead he continues and expands. He keeps talking about making room for nature in our hearts, about visceral contact we must have in order to love, and about falling in love with nature as with, if you wish, a wonderful guy. Then he recalls a banal soap opera, and, having switched back to cute girls (specifically, Mary Martin), ends his story with a tearful "Once you have found her/never let her go!" It seems that in this case, love for nature (or whatever it could be) has carried Gould a bit too far: all this comic drooling is over some snails so esoteric that Gould does not know their common names (he refers to them by their scientific, Latin name, *Partula*).

Another bizarre exhibition of alternative passions was published by College of Forestry of the Oregon University under the title "An erotics of place" (Williams 1995). While delivering a distinguished Starker Lecture, the author, "in the process of redefining our relationship to the land," talks about "dance with longing," arousal, asks questions like "what might it mean to make love with the land?" and complains that "this is taboo" (Williams 1995, p. 16-18). Both cases of biophilia came not from acknowledged psychopaths confined in a mental institution, but from esteemed people associated with respected centers of learning.

Gould's appeal may sound even more presumptuous for the poor people in the tropics who exterminate those species and environments. It is presumed that they have less developed emotional bonds with their native forests than visiting American professors. Can it be that these bonds are not a substitute for food? What are native people supposed to do in view of their hungry children and a middleman from a fast-food chain offering cash for beef? These people destroy forests together with millipedes and spiders not out of ignorance or malice. They simply want to eat and produce children who, again exclusively for their survival, will have to clear more land.

Ye Shall Make You No Idols

It would be overconfident to think that our discussion of the four criteria has exhausted the contents of ecosystem management or dispelled its charm. As are its ingredients, ecosystem management may be inexhaustible. Even when the answers to all these how's and where's are found wanting, ecosystem management can still be upheld on the basis of even higher arguments. Although writings on ecosystem management are replete with words like "scientific," "sound ecological models," "knowledge, more knowledge and cascades of knowledge," this new paradigm is more plausible in the realm of belief, rather than science. A perceptive testimony by Irland (1994, p. 17) goes to the heart of the problem: "We can make ecosystem management work if we believe in it."

This, at last, may well be true. However, since this conviction cannot be evaluated on a rational basis, it would be more appropriate to conduct its analysis in a theological journal.

SUSTAINABLE ENVIRONMENT
AND ECOSYSTEM MANAGEMENT

Even though the internal inconsistencies of goals and concepts of ecosystem management are of more than academic interest, they are still of limited significance as compared with the problem of a sustainable environment. This is the overriding issue of environmental management and, at present, of our civilization. Is it possible to expect that–despite the evidence that ecosystem management does not know what to manage (since biodiversity remains undefined), where to manage (we still cannot delineate the ecosystem, either), how to manage (approaches and techniques designed for a highly coordinated whole may be irrelevant to a largely haphazard potpourri, misnamed ecosystem), and why to manage (ecocentrism is suicidal; our ethics have to be anthropocentric)–this new management paradigm will lead us to the era of sustainable environment?

There are two approaches to attaining sustainability. One is to deal with the cause of environmental degradation, which is, as is widely recognized (Ehrlich 1988, Wilson 1992), our population and economic growth. Another approach is to attend to symptoms. This Journal stresses that to achieve sustainability "it is critical to deal with fundamental causes and not merely to respond to symptoms" (Berlyn and Ashton 1998, p. 154). Unfortunately, ecosystem management is restricted to treating symptoms of environmental decline. Ecosystem management deals with landscapes, wetlands, complex interactions, linkages, multiple scales, and extended time horizons. It is concerned with owls and thousands of endangered species. However, this new paradigm fails to address the crucial object–the single species that endangers the others and the environment as a whole. If the environment deteriorates now, it is not likely that it will be possible to achieve sustainability in the future when our numbers double and our standard of living will continue to grow–and grow.

Despite widespread admiration of ecosystem management and its main component, preserving biodiversity, one of their benefits remains unacknowledged. It is the benefit to our mental health. We realize that the ultimate cause of environmental degradation is our population and economic growth. Equally evident is our impotence to curb population growth in the developing countries and economic escalation everywhere in the world. To relieve the resulting frustration, we resort unconsciously to psychological defense mechanisms, which include an assortment of dodges such as rationalization, repression, regression, projection, and others. Biodiversity studies help us to recover our mental stability by redirecting the attention from unsolvable causes to manageable symptoms. Instead of anguishing over the impending population explosion that might wipe out our species, it may be wiser to pursue realistic though restricted targets, to save what is possible, "think globally, act locally," to do something tangible even on a small scale. This need is all too human and even more. In one of his many incisive statements, Leopold (1966, p. 186) described vividly this syndrome: "I had a bird dog named Gus. When Gus couldn't find pheasants he worked up an enthusiasm for Sora rails and meadowlarks. This whipped-up zeal for unsatisfactory substitutes masked his failure to find the real thing. It assuaged his inner frustration. We conservationists are like that."

Ecosystem management may be not only futile but damaging as well. If the judge who stopped tree harvesting in the Pacific Northwest looked deeper, he should prohibit house construction and printing newspapers. Then the forests would be preserved automatically. What happens after we succeed in relocating a dump or preventing the clear cutting of the spotted owl habitats? Until we stop growing, some other places must be degraded to satisfy the increasing demand for paper, timber, and dumping sites. Among these places some, such as tropical ecosystems, are likely to be more fragile than the Pacific Northwest forests. All proposals, recommendations, and suggestions for how the environment might be preserved or conserved are futile while our population and affluence keep increasing. If they are reduced, then ecosystem management would become unnecessary because the environment would be conserved and restored without any effort on our part.

Many things need to be done to achieve a sustainable environment. Dispelling attractive and well-meaning delusions is one of them.

LITERATURE CITED

Anonymous 1974. The Principal Laws Relating to Forest Service Activities. USDA, Forest Service Agriculture Handbook no 453.

Begon, M., J.L. Harper, and C.R. Townsend. 1996. Ecology. Third edition. Blackwell Science, London. 1068 p.

Berlyn, G.P. and P.M.S. Ashton. 1998. Forests and the ecosystem paradigm. Journal of Sustainable Forestry 7:141-157.

Boyce, M.S. and A. Haney, editors. 1997. Ecosystem management. Yale University Press, New Haven. 361 p.

Christensen, N.L. (Chair) 1996. The report of the Ecological Society of America Committee on the scientific basis for ecosystem management. Ecological Applications 6:659-691.

Cork, T.C. 1998. Land-use control through ecosystem management. Journal of Forestry 96(10):56.

Ehrlich, P.R. 1988. The loss of diversity: causes and consequences. Pages 21-27 in BioDiversity, edited by E.O. Wilson. National Academy Press, Washington, DC. 521 p.

Franklin, J.F. 1997. Ecosystem management: an overview. Pages 21-53 in Ecosystem management. Edited by M.S. Boyce and A. Haney. Yale University Press, New Haven. 361 p.

Gleason, H.A. 1926. The individualistic concept of the plant association. The New York Botanical Garden Contribution No. 279 as reprinted in Torrey Botanical Club Bulletin (1962) 53:7-26.

Golley, F.B. 1993. A history of the ecosystem concept in ecology. Yale University Press, New Haven. 254 p.

Gould, S.J. 1991. Unenchanted evening. Natural History, September, p. 4-14.

Haney, A. and M.S. Boyce. 1997. Introduction. Pages 1-17 in Ecosystem management. Edited by M.S. Boyce and A. Haney. Yale University Press, New Haven. 361 p.

Irland, L.C. 1994. Getting from here to there: implementing ecosystem management on the ground. Journal of Forestry 92(8):12-17.

Kaufman, M.R. et al. 1994. An ecological basis for ecosystem management. USDA Forest Service General Technical Report RM-246. 22 p.

Knight, R.L. 1996. Aldo Leopold, the land ethic, and ecosystem management. Journal of Wildlife Management 60(3):471-474.

Kuhn, T.S. 1970. The structure of scientific revolutions. 2d ed. University of Chicago Press, Chicago. 172 p.

Langhorst, D. 1999 . Biodiversity should be preserved. Pages 67-71 in L.K. Egendorf, editor. Conserving the Environment. Current Controversies. Greenhaven Press, San Diego, CA 208 p.

Leopold, A. 1966. A Sand County Almanac. Oxford University Press, New York. 269 p.

Lindeman, R.L. 1942. The trophic-dynamic aspect of ecology. Ecology 23:399-418.

Mendelsohn, R. 1994. A time of change: the past and the future of forestry. Pages 1-5 in Forest Economics on the Edge. D.H. Newman and M.E. Aronow, editors. The University of Georgia. 418 p.

Robertson, D. 1992. Memorandum. USDA Forest Service, June 4.

Tansley, A.G. 1935. The use and abuse of vegetational concepts and terms. Ecology 16:284-307.

Tarver, C.M. 1995. Ecosystem management: giving it meaning. Journal of Forestry 93(1):60.

Thomas, J.W. 1997. Foreword. Pages ix-xi in Ecosystem management edited by M.S. Boyce and A. Haney. Yale University Press, New Haven. 361 p.

Williams, T.T. 1995. An erotics of place. Pages 8-26 in Re-thinking natural resources. 1995 Starker Lectures. Compiled by B. Shelby and S. Arbogast. Oregon State University, Corvallis. 89 p.

Wilson, E.O. 1984. Biophilia. Harvard University Press, Cambridge, Massachusetts. 157 p.

Wilson, E.O. 1992. The diversity of life. Harvard University Press, Cambridge, Massachusetts. 424 p.

Wilson, E.O. 1994. Naturalist. Island Press, Washington, DC. 380 p.

Wilson, E.O. 1997. Introduction. Pages 1-3 in Biodiversity II, edited by M.L. Reaka-Kudla, D.E. Wilson, and E.O. Wilson. Joseph Henry Press, Washington, DC. 551 p.

Radically Contested Assertions
in Ecosystem Management

Robert T. Lackey

SUMMARY. Ecosystem management is a magnet for controversy, in part because some of its formulations rest on questionable assertions that are radically contested. These assertions are important to understanding much of the conflict surrounding ecosystem management and, therefore, deserve thoughtful discussion and vigorous debate. Unfortunately, the assertions usually receive little scrutiny because critics, supporters, and the public are, understandably, absorbed in the personal and societal consequences of implementing controversial public policy choices under the rubric of ecosystem management. Professional natural resource managers, typically operating from within government bureaucracies and professional organizations, tend to blunt debate over the critical assertions by depicting ecosystem management as an evolution of past management approaches. Others, usually from outside the traditional natural resource management professions, contend that ecosystem management is revolutionary, not evolutionary. In this more radical view, ecosystem management is much more than a mere reformulation of classic natural resource management. To accept such a radical view of ecosystem management, I propose that there are four necessary, but implicit assertions. None of the assertions is accepted without challenge: each has articulate supporters and detractors. My conclusion from evaluating the radically contested assertions and policy corollaries is that much, but not all, of what is alleged as a scientific basis for ecosystem management is an assertion of fundamen-

Robert T. Lackey is affiliated with National Health and Environmental Effects Research Laboratory, United States Environmental Protection Agency, 200 SW 35th Street, Corvallis, OR 97333.

[Haworth co-indexing entry note]: "Radically Contested Assertions in Ecosystem Management." Lackey, Robert T. Co-published simultaneously in *Journal of Sustainable Forestry* (Food Products Press, an imprint of The Haworth Press, Inc.) Vol. 9, No. 1/2, 1999, pp. 21-34; and: *Contested Issues of Ecosystem Management* (ed: Piermaria Corona, and Boris Zeide) Food Products Press, an imprint of The Haworth Press, Inc., 1999, pp. 21-34. Single or multiple copies of this article are available for a fee from The Haworth Document Delivery Service [1-800-342-9678, 9:00 a.m. - 5:00 p.m. (EST). E-mail address: getinfo@haworthpressinc.com].

tal values or, at the very least, an expression of personal policy prefer-ences. *[Article copies available for a fee from The Haworth Document Deliv-ery Service: 1-800-342-9678. E-mail address: getinfo@haworthpressinc.com <Website: http://www.haworthpressinc.com>]*

KEYWORDS. Ecosystem management, ecological policy, ecosystem health, forest management

INTRODUCTION

Ecosystem management has become a magnet for controversy (Fitzsimmons, 1996; Haeuber, 1996; Gilmore, 1997). On one side of the multi-sided debate, and reflecting a common view held by profes-sional natural resource managers, is a business-as-usual philosophy:

> I promise you that I can justify anything you want to do by saying it is ecosystem management. Not that I don't think it is a good idea. I applaud it. But right now it's incredibly nebulous. [Jack Ward Thomas, Chief of the U.S. Forest Service, speech to Forest Service public affairs personnel, April 11, 1993, as quoted in Fitzsimmons (1996)]

> The move to ecosystem management concepts is an evolutionary process that has been underway for decades and is becoming more and more feasible with developments in science, technolo-gy, and philosophy. The fuller embrace of the concept of ecosys-tem management is correctly identified as evolutionary as op-posed to revolutionary. (Thomas, 1996)

In marked contrast, ecosystem management represents to others nothing less than a fundamental change in social policy:

> The philosophy of ecosystem management requires asking our-selves what kind of a society, and correspondingly, what kind of relationship with nature we want. Patterns of politics suggested by ecosystem management include public deliberation of values toward the environment, cooperative solutions, and dispersion of power and authority. These are all avenues to lessen social hierar-chy and domination. Through opening the value debate, fostering

a sense of interdependence among humans, and renewing a sense of reason, the chains of social domination may be lessened. (Wallace et al., 1996)

Another set of proponents view society's adoption of ecosystem management as a fundamental shift in values, ethics, and morals:

A human community in a sustainable relationship with a nonhuman community is based on the following precepts: first, equity between the human and nonhuman communities; second, moral consideration for both humans and other species; third, respect for both cultural diversity and biodiversity; fourth, inclusion of women, minorities, and nonhuman nature in the code of ethical accountability; and fifth, that ecologically sound management is consistent with the continued health of both the human and the nonhuman communities. (Merchant, 1997)

Still others pattern their vision of ecosystem management as reaching a higher stage of human consciousness:

Ecosystem management defines a paradigm that weaves biophysical and social threads into a tapestry of beauty, health, and sustainability. It embraces both social and ecological dynamics in a flexible and adaptive process. Ecosystem management celebrates the wisdom of both our minds and hearts, and lights our path to the future. (Cornett, 1994)

Formulations of ecosystem management that purport to "lessen social hierarchy and domination" or call for "moral consideration for both humans and other species" or celebrate "the wisdom of both our minds and hearts, and lights our path to the future" do not sound like business-as-usual. Admitting that a natural resource manager "can justify anything you want to do by saying it is ecosystem management" would, however, support the precept that ecosystem management is so vague a concept as to be operationally meaningless.

ASSERTIONS

The more revolutionary formulations of ecosystem management that purport to be a radical shift in public policy rest on several fundamental postulates–what may be termed radically contested, or highly questionable, assertions. How these assertions are adjudicated will determine whether the label "ecosystem management" connotes business-as-usual or a fundamental shift in ecological policy. It is the assertions that are important in interpreting most of the conflict swirling around ecosystem management.

Unfortunately, the assertions usually receive little formal or coherent scrutiny–mainly because critics, supporters, and the public are, understandably, absorbed in the personal and societal consequences of implementing controversial public policy choices under the rubric of ecosystem management. The assertions are rarely articulated and debates often center around elements of scientific understanding.

Further inhibiting debate over the critical assertions is the tendency by professional natural resource managers and scientists (especially in the fisheries, forestry, and wildlife disciplines), operating from within government bureaucracies and professional organizations, to steer ecosystem management toward being simply an evolutionary stage of the well-established natural resource management paradigm:

> Ecosystem management is not a rejection of the anthropocentric for a totally biocentric world view. Rather, it is management that acknowledges the importance of human needs while at the same time confronting the reality that the capacity of our world to meet those needs in perpertuity has limits and depends on the function of ecosystems. (Christensen et al., 1995)

> . . . there is no *a priori* imperative to include management for biodiversity, ecosystem health and integrity, and commodity production in every ecosystem-management effort, and therefore to specify them in a general definition. (Wagner, 1995)

In such a bureaucratic reformulation and redefinition by experts, ecosystem management becomes merely a contemporary description of the time-honored natural resource management paradigm where society's values and preferences change (as professional natural resource managers presume) and the process of natural resource management (ecosystem management) incorporates such changes (Lackey, 1998). There is nothing deceitful or diabolic with such efforts to depict ecosystem management in terms of a classically technocratic approach to implementing ecological policy, but it does blunt much of the moral and political passion underlying many formulations of ecosystem management.

In spite of pervasive efforts by government bureaucracies and natural resource professionals to appropriate the jargon of ecosystem management to describe an evolution of the traditional natural resources management paradigm (Fitzsimmons, 1996, 1998; Thomas, 1996), some proponents (Merchant, 1997; Wallace et al., 1996) claim, usually outside the professional venues of natural resource managers and scientists, that ecosystem management is revolutionary, not evolutionary, and it is much more than a mere reformulation of the classic natural resource management paradigm. But the revolution/evolution split is not articulated because it is usually uncertain whether the participants are arguing over technical or administrative implementation, or are debating a fundamentally different set of premises. Also masking the fundamental issues is that the same words often are used with very different meanings.

My purpose is to identify the fundamental premises upon which the revolutionary view of ecosystem management is based. After reviewing the recent literature (both formally published and the many dialogs and debates held on computer list servers), I propose that there are four implicit assertions that constitute the underpinning of the revolutionary view of ecosystem management. Each of the assertions leads directly to an ecological policy corollary that, if accepted, would have major ramifications on public policy and natural resources management. None of the assertions is accepted unchallenged; each has eloquent supporters and detractors, but all continue to be radically contested.

Assertion 1–Ecosystems Are Real

Policy Corollary–Ecosystems Can and Should Be Managed

What is an ecosystem? The easy answer is a generic text definition, but these definitions are so general as to be of limited use in management (Fitzsimmons, 1998). In practice, however, ecosystems are defined at scales from a drop of morning dew to an ocean, from a mountain meadow to a continent, or from a pebble to a planet. Thus, there are things, systems, we commonly call ecosystems, but their scale is determined by the management problem at hand. Must we be constrained to deal in specifics when defining and bounding ecosystems? If dew drops and continents legitimately may be defined as ecosystems, then what practical value is added by using the ecosystem concept in decision making?

Perhaps there are other "ecosystem" concepts that might delimit boundaries and thus be useful in management or policy analysis. One possibility is the "watershed." Watersheds have fairly discrete boundaries but a scale must first be defined. As with ecosystems, scale may range from a few meters to millions of kilometers. Another possibility is use of the term "ecoregion." Ecoregions, however, are only tolerably discrete once the attributes of an ecoregion are codified. As with ecosystems and watersheds, the attributes of ecoregions are context (problem) specific.

Thus, the boundaries or definition of ecosystems in ecosystem management (and watersheds or ecoregions) are entirely derived from the specific management or policy question being addressed. There are no general characteristics of ecosystems that are useful in setting specific boundaries *a priori.* In short, ecosystems are, and will always be, entirely context specific.

Because there are no *a priori* boundaries for ecosystems in the absence of a particular policy or management question, the central issues become: (1) what is the policy or management problem at hand? and (2) who has a mandate to adjudicate among competing visions of the policy or management question? For example, is ecosystem management limited to managing public forest lands? Such a rigorously constrained definition of the management focus (public forest lands) simplifies policy and ecological analysis, but who decides that such a narrow focus is appropriate? Or should ecosystem management focus on ecosystem boundaries independent of ownership? Why the apparent focus on publicly owned forest lands? Are not urbanized areas equally relevant and appropriately included within the boundaries of ecosystems?

The assertion that ecosystems are real must be accompanied by the caveat that ecosystems are real only in the sense that a specific management, policy, or scientific problem has been articulated, thus permitting the ecological boundaries (the ecosystem) of concern to be delimited. Accepting the assertion that ecosystems are real means that someone has defined the management, policy, or scientific problem–that is, set the relative values and preferences of concern.

If the assertion that ecosystems are real (in a policy or management sense) is accepted, then the policy corollary (*"ecosystems can and should be managed"*) is a logical adjunct. Because ecosystems are defined in a policy or management context, the significant public debate should be over delineation of the policy problem to be solved. Once the policy problem (or societal goal) is defined, the ecosystem boundaries will probably be deduced with relative ease because it is largely a scientific exercise.

Thus, the assertion that *"ecosystems are real"* is tenuous. The corollary *"ecosystems can and should be managed"* is only true once the policy or management goal is defined and accepted. Having articulated the policy or management goal, the ecosystem includes all the ecological components necessary to meet the goal.

Assertion 2–Natural and Undisturbed Is Inherently Preferable to Altered and Disturbed

Policy Corollary–Native Species Are Inherently More Important Than Exotic Species and, Therefore, Biological Diversity Should Not Be Reduced

Though not clearly stated, in many formulations of ecosystem management there is a tacit assertion that natural ecosystems are inherently preferable to unnatural (or human altered) ecosystems. Some are more direct, bluntly stating that "Ecosystem management is a response to today's deepening biodiversity crisis" or declaring that ecosystem management has ". . . the general goal of protecting native ecosystem integrity over the long term" (Grumbine, 1994). "Integrity" is, by definition, based on native species and native ecosystems. By implication, man's activities are inherently bad or adverse. Perhaps there is an admission that humans need the products and services of ecosystems to survive, much less prosper, but it is almost as if this need was an unfortunate but unavoidable reality. Even in bureaucratic formulations of ecosystem management, terms such as "degradation," "health," and "impoverishment" imply that the benchmark for ecosystems is no disturbance, and that human disturbance results in some degree of "degradation," something less than optimal "health," and a reduction in biotic "richness."

Another area in which assertions of preferences arise is in definitions of what appear to be scientific terms. For example, what is meant by ecological integrity? A typical answer is provided by Westra

(1996a): "An ecosystem can be said to possess integrity when it is wild; that is, free as much as possible today from human intervention. It is an 'unmanaged' ecosystem, although not necessarily a pristine one." The word *integrity* typically connotes "goodness" or "desirability." Therefore, human intervention must, by definition, reduce integrity.

The importance placed on the pedigree of the species present in an area also shows a common acceptance of the policy corollary that native species are more important than exotic species. Exotic species may be called ". . . the Gestapo of ecology" (Windsor, 1998), but usually their status is less obviously stated. For example, exotic species are routinely excluded in measuring biological diversity. Why are native species more important than exotic species? Further, among the exotic species, why are intentional introductions usually treated differently than unintentional introductions relative to biological diversity? Should the same ideas apply to humans? *Homo sapiens* in North America, for example, was (or is) an exotic species.

Individuals and society may value certain species more than others or it may value all species equally, but such valuations are societal preferences, not scientific judgements. In fact, concepts such as biological diversity reflect an element of societal preference, as well as scientific understanding. However, the use of a scientific imperative to justify protecting biological diversity is an example of mythology (Ghilarov, 1996). Whether society prefers "natural and undisturbed" ecosystems to "altered and disturbed" is purely a societal judgement. There is nothing inherent in science that makes either pristine or altered ecosystems inherently preferable from a policy standpoint.

Assertion 3–Everything Is Connected to Everything Else

Policy Corollary–Ecosystem Management Is Best Done Within Large Geographical Areas

There is a tantalizing appeal to the premise that everything in nature, and all of ecological policy for that matter, is related to everything else. After all, the air currents caused by a single butterfly flapping his wings once could plausibly be the stimulus for a hurricane on the other side of the earth, but no one can predict *a priori* the consequences of a butterfly flapping his wings. Scientists and analysts must simplify problems in science and policy at their peril or they cannot predict anything with confidence.

The reality in decision analysis is that some simplifications must be made or it is impossible to conduct any credible scientific or policy analysis. The question is how much simplification is warranted. For example, all decisions are constrained by boundaries, physical, biological, and social. Boundaries must be applied to decision problems (or scientific analyses) in order to make analytical work tractable. The tradeoff at the extremes is between scientific rigor (e.g., simple physical, chemical, or biological models) that has limited direct policy relevance and more complete models (e.g., computer simulations of complex systems) that are more realistic in a policy sense, but are not credible scientifically.

What about arguments for "holistic" or "bioregional" management that are advanced by some proponents of ecosystem management? Such arguments may have a superficial appeal, but the issue is where the boundaries are drawn, not whether policy problems are "holistic" or not. It may be difficult to be against holistic approaches, but where does society draw policy or scientific boundaries–a population of deer, a local watershed, an ecoregion, a biome, a continent, the planet? In practice the boundary must be set somewhere, otherwise ecosystem management will sink into flowery rhetoric, and not be useful in solving societal problems.

Some implicitly argue that the policy corollary to "everything is related to everything else" is that boundaries ought to delimit very large areas–implicitly accepting that the policy problems of concern are best addressed over large regions. What scale? Bioregional scales are popular in much of the literature, but who defines policy questions that justify boundaries at such a geographic level? Studying ecological problems over large regions has a certain scientific rationale, but it does not follow that government "management" programs work well across large regions.

The policy and social implications of implementing ecosystem management within large geographic areas would potentially be a sea change in ecological policy. As Cortner and Moote (1994) observe:

> A paradigm shift to actual ecosystem-level management will not be possible under the existing management structure, which divides land and water along political boundaries and sections ecosystems into commodity resources.

Political boundaries may sound innocuous to the casual reader, but Cortner and Moote go on to elaborate that professional natural resource managers must, in order to implement ecosystem management, adopt ". . . a radical revision of our own values, management practices, and institutional structures. . . ." Is such a requisite fundamental shift in thought acknowledgment that ecosystem management requires greater government over private property? The answer offered by Fitzsimmons (1998) is explicit:

> Full implementation of a policy of federal management and protection of ecosystems would extend the reach of federal regulators to all private land in the United States, increase regulatory burdens, and further restrict the economic use of public and private lands.

Assertion 4–There Is a Moral Imperative for Ecosystem Management

Policy Corollary–The Benefits and Costs of Decisions in Ecosystem Management Are Accruable to All Ecosystem Components, Not Solely to Humans

No aspect of the debate over the proper interpretation of ecosystem management is more crucial than the assertion that there is a moral imperative for its implementation. For example, in discussing the philosophical and moral basis for managing natural resources, Westra (1996b) concludes with an opinion on the role of citizen choice relative to a larger philosophical and moral mandate:

> Thus, no country's unilateral decisions, no matter how representative it might be of its citizens' values, should be permitted to prevail, unless it does not conflict with the global requirements of the ethics of integrity, thus with true sustainability.

Exactly what is the moral imperative to protect ecological integrity, an imperative that is often a cornerstone of ecosystem management? Who defines it? At least for the question of who defines integrity, there is one obvious answer offered by proponents: scientists. Being anointed with the mandate to define ecological integrity conveys an enormous influence in disputes over ecological policy. In evaluating the role of scientists within such a policy context, Sagoff (1995) observed:

To be sure, both community and systems ecology retained faith with the central thesis of the Great Chain of Being that nature exemplifies a timeless and intelligible order rather than sheer historical contingency. By secularizing this religious intuition, however, ecosystem science replaces a priesthood of theologians with one of engineers and mathematical modelers.

As best I can untangle it, the alleged moral imperative for ecosystem management is that humans are entrusted with protecting the world. There may be an implicit policy corollary that all species are equal and that each should be treated properly: species or individuals other than humans should be considered in ecosystem management beyond their role in achieving human benefits. The obvious competing moral imperative is that benefits from decisions in ecosystem management are accruable only to humans. It follows from this human-centered assertion that society may wish to safeguard natural ecosystems, sustain all species, preserve all populations, shield from harm all individual mammals, birds, and fish, or hold entire continents free of human habitation. But the reason that society might do these things, if the human-centered moral imperative is accepted, is because the benefits to humans are worth the costs.

There is, of course, nothing wrong with asserting a moral imperative for ecosystem management except that the world is made up of competing moral imperatives. Nor can ecology or any other scientific discipline help much in resolving the debates because science and scientific information deals with the "what is" questions and not the "what ought to be" questions. Consider, for example, the question of whether a wetland should be preserved? Converting a swamp to a corn field, university campus, or parking lot has ecological consequences which must be determined scientifically, but whether we want the wetland, soybean field, university campus, or parking lot is a societal decision.

Assertions of moral imperatives are not limited to formulations of ecosystem management. Heilig (1997), for example, concludes a critical analysis of ecological policy in general and sustainable development in particular with:

> We should be aware that the sustainability concept until now has mainly been a social philosophy, packed with hidden assumptions, values, and lifestyle ideals. Popular among sustainability

advocates is the Calvinistic 'slow-down' philosophy: we should limit our traveling, our eating of red meat; we should lower the temperature in our apartments, and use bicycles instead of cars.

The assertion that there is a moral imperative for ecosystem management (essentially that benefits and costs of decisions are accruable to all ecosystem components) is a radical concept. Scientists and scientific information are not relevant in determining the acceptability of such an assertion. A formulation based on such an assertion would be revolutionary in concept and application. (My guess is, however, that many of the proponents of such a moral imperative tacitly accept the more traditional human-centered assertion [benefits are accruable to humans], but they place much higher relative value on ecosystems, species, or individual nonhuman plants and animal survival than the average citizen.) The debate has the character of an argument over a human-centered management vs. a bioegalitarian paradigm, but the debate is really over the relative importance of alternative benefits (e.g, paper vs. spotted owls, hamburger vs. wolves, electricity vs. white water rafting, etc.).

CONCLUSION

After evaluating the radically contested assertions and policy corollaries of ecosystem management, I conclude that much, but not all, of what is proclaimed as a scientific basis for ecosystem management is, at its heart, an assertion of fundamental values. At the very least, the claimed scientific basis for ecosystem management is an expression of personal policy preferences. To fairly characterize ecosystem management or to debate its appropriateness as a public policy paradigm, it is essential to clearly separate those elements of the paradigm that should be driven by science from those components that should be based on individual or societal values and preferences.

It is fallacious to say that ecosystem management, or the traditional natural resources management paradigm, should be science-driven. Rather, it is more accurate to say that ecosystem management is dependent on, but constrained by, science and scientific information. Regardless of how ecosystem management may be defined and which, if any, radically contested assertions are invoked, a key role of ecological (scientific) information is to identify the limits or constraints that bound the options to achieve various societal, or in some formulations of ecosystem management, *non*societal, benefits. Ecological information is important in implementing effective ecosystem management (or any alternative management paradigm), even though it is only one ingredient in the decision-making process that should be driven largely on public or private choices.

There appear to be two policy trajectories for resolving the operational meaning of ecosystem management. The first, and most likely to happen, is that the expression "ecosystem management" might be defined as functionally equivalent to the classic natural resource management paradigm and merely reflects another stage in evolving societal values and preferences. The other path is that "ecosystem management" will come to be the policy banner for an eco-centered world-view closely tied to concepts of species egalitarianism, bioregionalism, democratization, and possibly local empowerment.

In spite of the scientific character of much of the debate over ecosystem management, most of the divisive issues are not scientific: they are most often clashes over moral and philosophical positions or different individual preferences. In the absence of a societal consensus on the radically contested assertions I have described, it will be extremely difficult to harmonize the divisive issues in ecosystem management. Stated in a more pragmatic context, the policy debate in ecosystem management will continue to be who or what wins and who or what loses and over what period of time.

Ecosystem management remained relatively free of controversy as long as it was defined in sufficiently general terms so that nearly anyone's policy position plausibly could be accommodated. Efforts to demand precision of thought, however, have forced deep-seated moral, philosophical, and economic divisions to the surface. Rather than be judged a political platitude that offends no one, ecosystem management has become a lightning rod for controversy in public policy.

LITERATURE CITED

Cornett, Zane J. 1994. Ecosystem management: why now? *Ecosystem Management News*, USDA Forest Service. 3(14): no page numbers.

Cortner, Hanna J., and Margaret A. Moote. 1994. Trends and issues in land and water resources management: setting the agenda for change. *Environmental Management*. 18(2): 167-173.

Christensen, Norman L., et al. 1995. The report of the Ecological Society of America

Committee on the Scientific Basis for Ecosystem Management. *Ecological Applications*. 6(3): 665-691.

Fitzsimmons, Allan K. 1996. Sound policy or smoke and mirrors: does ecosystem management make sense? *Water Resources Bulletin*. 32(2): 217-227.

Fitzsimmons, Allan K. 1998. Why a policy of federal management and protection of ecosystems is a bad idea. *Landscape and Urban Planning*. 40(1/3): 195-202.

Ghilarov, Alexej. 1996. What does 'biodiversity' mean–scientific problem or convenient myth? *Trends in Ecology and Evolution*. 11(7): 304-306.

Gilmore, Daniel W. 1997. Ecosystem management–a needs drive, resource-use philosophy. *The Forest Chronicle*. 73(5): 560-564.

Grumbine, R. Edward. 1994. What is ecosystem management? *Conservation Biology*. 8: 27-38.

Haeuber, Richard. 1996. The case of ecosystem management. *Natural Resources Journal*. 36: 1-28.

Heilig, Gerhard K. 1997. Sustainable development–ten arguments against a biologistic 'slow-down' philosophy of social and economic development. *International Journal of Sustainable Development and World Ecology*. 4: 1-16.

Lackey, Robert T. 1998. Seven pillars of ecosystem management. *Landscape and Urban Planning*. 40(1/3): 21-30.

Merchant, Carolyn. 1997. Fist first!: the changing ethics of ecosystem management. *Human Ecology Review*. 4(1): 25-30.

Sagoff, Mark. 1995. The value of integrity. Chapter 11 in *Perspectives on Ecological Integrity*, Laura Westra and J. Lemons, editors, Kluwer Academic Publishers, pp. 162-176.

Thomas, Jack W. 1996. Forest service perspective on ecosystem management. *Ecological Applications*. 6(3): 703-705.

Wagner, Frederic H. 1995. What have we learned? *Ecosystem Management of Natural Resources in the Intermountain West*, Natural Resources and Environmental Issues, Volume 5, pp. 121-125.

Wallace, Mary G., Hanna J. Cortner, Margaret A. Moote, and Sabrina Burke. 1996. Moving toward ecosystem management: examining a change in philosophy for resource management. *Journal of Political Ecology*. 3: 1-36.

Westra, Laura. 1996a. Environmental integrity, racism, and health. *The Science of the Total Environment*. 184: 57-66.

Westra, Laura. 1996b. Ecosystem integrity and the "fish wars." *Journal Aquatic Ecosystem Health*. 5: 275-282.

Windsor, Donald A. 1998. The Endangered Species Act is analogous to Schindler's List. *Conservation Biology*. 12(2): 485-486.

Population Growth, Environmental Resources and Global Food

David Pimentel
Marcia Pimentel

SUMMARY. Rapid growth in the world population threatens agricultural and forestry production. Currently, there are 6 billion people on earth, and we add a quarter million more each day. There are more than 3 billion people malnourished in the world at present–the largest number and proportion ever in history. Land, water and biological resources are being degraded at an alarming rate; this degradation has substantial negative impacts on food and forest production. *[Article copies available for a fee from The Haworth Document Delivery Service: 1-800-342-9678. E-mail address: getinfo@haworthpressinc.com <Website: http://www.haworthpressinc.com>]*

KEYWORDS. Population, natural resources, ecology, food

INTRODUCTION

Food shortages exist because the human population is increasing faster than the food production capability of the world's agricultural

---

David Pimentel and Marcia Pimentel are affiliated with the College of Agriculture and Life Sciences, Division of Nutritional Sciences, 5126 Comstock Hall, Cornell University, Ithaca, NY 14853-0901.

[Haworth co-indexing entry note]: "Population Growth, Environmental Resources and Global Food." Pimentel, David, and Marcia Pimentel. Co-published simultaneously in *Journal of Sustainable Forestry* (Food Products Press, an imprint of The Haworth Press, Inc.) Vol. 9, No. 1/2, 1999, pp. 35-44; and: *Contested Issues of Ecosystem Management* (ed: Piermaria Corona, and Boris Zeide) Food Products Press, an imprint of The Haworth Press, Inc., 1999, pp. 35-44. Single or multiple copies of this article are available for a fee from The Haworth Document Delivery Service [1-800-342-9678, 9:00 a.m. - 5:00 p.m. (EST). E-mail address: getinfo@haworthpressinc.com].

system. Uneven distribution of food, inability to afford food, and even political unrest all threaten world food security.

In the world today, more than 3 billion humans–50% of the population–are currently considered malnourished; this is the largest number and proportion of hungry humans ever recorded in history (WHO, 1996)! Based on current rates of increase, the world population is projected to double to more than 12 billion in less than 50 years (PRB, 1997). At a time when the world population continues to expand at a rate of 1.5%/year (adding more than a quarter million people daily), providing adequate food becomes an increasingly difficult problem. The number of malnourished people could conceivably reach 4 to 5 billion in future decades.

Reports from the Food and Agricultural Organization of the United Nations and the U.S. Department of Agriculture, as well as from numerous other international organizations, further confirm the serious situation for global supply (NAS, 1994). For example, the *per capita* availability of world cereal grains, which make up 80% of the world's food supply, has been declining since 1983 (Kendall and Pimentel, 1994). These shortages are now reflected in major increases in the price of cereal grains, the basic food for billions of people (USDA, 1996).

Thus, as the world population continues to expand, more pressure than ever before is placed on all the basic resources that are essential for food production. Unfortunately, while the human population grows exponentially, food production can only increase linearly. Nevertheless, degradation of land, water, energy, and biological resources vital to agriculture continues unabated, further limiting the world's food production capability (Pimentel et al., 1998a).

AGRICULTURAL RESOURCES

More than 99% of the world's food supply comes from the land, while less than 1% is harvested from oceans or other aquatic habitats (FAO, 1991; Pimentel et al., 1998a). The production of an adequate food supply is directly dependent on ample quantities of fertile land, fresh water, energy sources, and natural biodiversity. Obviously, as the human population grows, the requirements for all these resources will increase as well. Even if these resources are never completely depleted, over time their supply will decline significantly on a per capita basis, because the finite amount of resources must be divided among more and more people.

Cropland. Throughout the world, fertile cropland for all types of crops is currently being lost from production at an alarming rate. This loss is illustrated by the diminishing amount of land now devoted to cereal grains (Pimentel et al., 1995). Soil erosion by both wind and water, as well as simple overuse, are responsible for the loss of about 30% of the world cropland during the past 40 years (WRI, 1994; Pimentel et al., 1995). Once fertile soil is lost, it takes 500 years or more to form a mere 25 mm of new, usable soil. For crop production, at least 150 mm of fertile soil is required.

This eroded and unproductive agricultural land is being replaced primarily by cleared forest land and/or marginal quality agricultural land. The need for more agricultural land accounts for more than 60% of the world's deforestation (Myers, 1994). And even despite such drastic land replacement strategies, world cropland per capita is still declining. Per capita cropland currently stands at only 0.27 ha per capita, about 50% of the 0.5 ha per capita considered the minimum for the production of a healthy, diverse diet (similar to that typical diet in the United States and Europe) (Lal and Stewart, 1990; Pimentel et al., 1998a). China has only 0.08 ha per capita, or about 15% of the accepted minimum amount (Pimentel et al., 1998a).

Forest Land. Forest resources are essential to many people in the world for cooking and preparing food. In developing countries, it takes about 2 kcal of wood to cook each 1 kcal of food (Pimentel et al., 1997b). All in all, each person in these developing countries depends on about 700 kg of woodfuel per person for both cooking and heat.

Currently in the United States each person utilizes about 1 hectare of land for forest resources; worldwide, this average is 0.75, and some places, is even lower. In China, for example, the average per capita use of forest resources is 0.11 ha (Pimentel et al., 1998a). During the last decade, per capita forest land has declined by about 25%; unfortunately, as the world population continues to grow and deforestation increases, the amount of forest land available per person continues to decrease (Pimentel et al., 1997b).

Water. Rainfall and its collection in rivers, lakes, and vast underground aquifers provides the water needed by humans for their survival and diverse activities.

Fresh water is critical for all vegetation including crops. All use and transpire massive amounts of water during the growing season. For example, a hectare of corn, producing about 8,000 kg/ha, will transpire more than 5 million liters of water during one growing season (Pimentel et al., 1997a). This means that more than 8 million liters of water must reach each hectare of corn during the growing season. In total, agricultural production consumes more fresh water than any other human activity. Specifically, about 70% of the world's fresh water supply is consumed, that is used up by agriculture and thus, is unavailable for other uses (Postel, 1996).

Water resources are under great stress as populous cities, states, and countries increase their withdrawal of water from rivers, lakes, and aquifers every year. For example, by the time the Colorado River reaches Mexico it has almost disappeared before it finally trickles into the Gulf of California (Sheridan, 1983; Postel, 1996). Also, the great Ogalla aquifer in the central U.S. is suffering an overdraft rate that is about 140% above recharge rate (Gleick, 1993). Water shortages in the U.S. and elsewhere in the world already are reflected in the per capita decline in crop irrigation during the past twenty years (Postel, 1996).

To compound the water problem, about 40% of the world population live in regions that directly compete for shared water resources (Gleick, 1993). In China, for example, more than 300 cities already are short of water, and these shortages are intensifying as Chinese urban areas expand (WRI, 1994). Competition for water resources among individuals, industries, regions both within and between countries is growing throughout the world community (Gleick, 1993).

Along with the quantity of water, its purity also is important. Diseases, associated with impure water and unsanitary systems rob people of their health, nutrients, and livelihood. These problems are most serious in developing countries, where about 90 per cent of the diseases can be traced to a lack of pure water (WHO, 1992; Pimentel et al., 1998b). Worldwide, about 4 billion cases of disease are contracted from impure water and approximately 6 million deaths are caused by water-borne disease each year (Pimentel et al., 1998b). Furthermore, when a person is stricken with diarrhea, malaria, or other serious disease, from 5 to 20 percent of an individual's food intake is used by the body to offset the stress of the disease further, diminishing the benefits of his/her food (Pimentel et al., 1998b).

Disease and malnutrition problems appear to be particularly serious, in the third world where poverty and poor sanitation is endemic

(Shetty and Shetty, 1993). The number of people living in urban areas is doubling every 10 to 20 years, creating other environmental problems, including the lack of water and sanitation, increased air pollution plus increased food shortages. For these reasons, the potential for the spread of disease is great in urban areas (Science, 1995).

Energy. Energy from many sources, most importantly fossil energy, is a prime resource used in food production. About 75% of the fossil energy used throughout the world each year is consumed by populations living in developed countries. Of this, about 17% is expended in the production, processing, and packaging of food products (Pimentel and Pimentel, 1996). The intensive farming technologies characteristic of develop*ed* countries rely on massive amounts of fossil energy for fertilizers, pesticides, irrigation, and for machines that substitute for human labor. In contrast, develop*ing* countries use fossil energy primarily for fertilizers and irrigation to help maintain yields, rather than to reduce human labor inputs (Giampietro and Pimentel, 1993).

The world supply of oil is projected to last approximately 50 years at current production rates (Campbell, 1997; Duncan, 1997; Youngquist, 1997; Duncan and Youngquist, 1998; Kerr, 1998). Worldwide, the natural gas supply is adequate for about 50 years and coal for about 100 years (Youngquist, 1997). These projections, however, are based on current consumption rates and current population numbers; these energy supplies could diminish even more rapidly if population and/or consumption continue to rise.

Youngquist (1997) reports that current oil and gas exploration drilling data has not borne out some of the earlier optimistic estimates of the amount of these resources yet to be found in the United States. Both the production rate and proved reserves have continued to decline. Reliable analyses suggest that at present (1998) the United States has consumed about three-quarters of the recoverable oil that was ever in the ground, and that we are currently rapidly consuming the last 25% of our oil resources (Bartlett, 1998). It is projected that U.S. domestic oil and natural gas production will be substantially less in 20 years than it is today. Even now, the current oil supply is not sufficient to meet domestic needs, and oil is imported in increasing yearly amounts (Youngquist, 1997). Importing 60% of its oil puts the United States economy at risk due to fluctuating oil prices and difficult political situations, such as those that occurred in the 1973 oil crisis and the 1991 Gulf War (U.S. Congressional Record, 1997).

Biodiversity. A productive and sustainable agricultural system, indeed the quality of human life, also depends on maintaining the integrity of natural biodiversity that exists on earth. Often small in size, diverse species serve as natural enemies to control pests, help degrade wastes, improve soil quality, fix nitrogen for plants, pollinate crops and other vegetation, and provide numerous other vital services for humans and their environment (Pimentel et al., 1997c). Consider that one-third of all crops worldwide require insect pollination. Humans have no technology to substitute for the pollination task, or for many of the other contributions provided by the estimated 10 million species that inhabit the earth (Pimentel et al., 1997c). Maintaining the diverse species that contribute to and carry out these important tasks is vitally important.

Food Distribution. Some people assume that market mechanisms and international trade are effective insurances against future food shortages. However, when the biological and physical limits of domestic food production are reached by all nations, food importation will no longer be a viable option for any country; at that point, food importation for rich countries will only be sustained by starvation of the poor. In the final analysis, the existing biological and physical resource constraints regulate and limit all food production systems.

Two observations support these concerns about the future. First, most of the 183 nations of the world are now dependent on food imports. Most of these are cereal grain imports. These grains are imported from countries that now have relatively low population densities, where intensive agriculture is practiced and where surpluses are common. For instance, the United States, Canada, Australia, France, and Argentina provide about 80% of the cereal exports on the world market (WRI, 1992). This situation is expected to change, though, when the U.S. population doubles in the next 60 years (as is expected based on the current population growth rate [USBC, 1996]). Then, countries like the U.S. will no longer have grain surpluses; instead of exporting cereals and other food resources, these foods will have to be retained domestically to feed 540 million hungry Americans. The United States, along with other exporting countries, will cease to be a food exporting country.

In the future, when the four major exporting countries retain surpluses for home use, Egypt, Jordan, and countless other countries in Africa and Asia will be without food imports that are basic to their survival. China, which now imports many tons of food, illustrates the severity of this problem. If, as Brown (1995) predicts, China's population increases by 500 million beyond their present 1.2 billion, and their soil erosion continues unabated, it will need to import 200-400 million tons of food grains each year starting in 2050. This minimal quantity is equal to more than the current grain exports of *all* the exporter nations mentioned earlier (USBC, 1996). Based on realistic trends, sufficient food supplies probably will not be available for import by China or any other nation on the international market to import by 2050 (Brown, 1995).

Technology. Over time, technology has been instrumental in increasing industrial and agricultural production, improving transportation and communications, advancing human health care, and in general, improving many aspects of human life. However, much of its success is based on the availability of the natural resources of the earth.

In no area is this more evident than in agricultural production. No known or future technology will be able to double the world's amount of arable land. Granted, technologically produced fertilizers are effective in enhancing the fertility of eroded croplands, but their production relies on the diminishing supply of fossil fuels. In fact, fertilizer use per capita during the past decade has decreased 23% and continues to decline (IFDC, 1998).

The increase in the size and speed of fishing vessels has not resulted in increases in per capita fish catch (Pimentel and Pimentel, 1996). For example, in regions like eastern Canada, over-fishing has become so severe that about 80,000 fisherman have no fish to catch, and the entire industry has been lost (W. Rees, University of British Columbia, personal communication, 1996).

Consider also the world supplies of fresh water that are available must be shared by more individuals, and for increased agriculture and industry. No available technology can double the flow of the Colorado River; the shrinking ground water resources in vast aquifers cannot be refilled by human technology. Rainfall is the only supplier of water.

Certainly, improved technology will help increase food production, by the more effective management and use of resources. However, technology cannot produce an unlimited flow of those vital natural resources that are the raw material for sustained agricultural production. Even presently available technology is not being employed adequately, as cereal grain production per capita has been declining since 1983 and continues to decline?

Biotechnology has the potential for some advances in agriculture, provided the ability to transfer genetic material is wisely used. However, the developments in biotechnology from more than 20 years ago have not stemmed the decline in per capita food production during the past 15 years. Currently, about 40% of the research effort in biotechnology is devoted to the development of herbicide resistance in crops (Paoletti and Pimentel, 1996). This technology will not increase crop yields, but it will increase the use of chemical herbicides and the pollution of the environment.

WHAT OF THE FUTURE?

We can not ignore the fact that per capita food production has been declining for more than a decade, nor the fact that more than 3 billion people are currently malnourished. Related to this decline in food production are simultaneous decreases in the per capita availability of the following resources: Forest land, 25%; fertilizers, 23%; cropland, 20%; irrigation, 12%; and fish, 10%. Strategies for global food security must be based first and foremost on the conservation and careful management of the land, water, energy, and biological resources required for food production. Our stewardship of world resources will have to change. The basic needs of all people must be brought into balance with the availability of life-sustaining natural resources. The conservation of these resources will require the coordinated efforts of all individuals and countries. Once these finite resources are exhausted they cannot be replaced by human technology. In addition, more efficient and environmentally sound agricultural technologies must be developed and put into practice to support the continued productivity of agriculture (Pimentel and Pimentel, 1996).

Unfortunately, none of these conservation measures will be sufficient to ensure adequate food supplies for future generations unless the growth in the human population is simultaneously curtailed. Several studies have confirmed that to enjoy a relatively high standard of living, the optimum human population should be less than 200 million for the U.S. and less than 2 billion for the world (Pimentel et al., 1998a). This harsh projection assumes, that from now until such an optimum population is achieved, *all* strategies for the conservation of soil, water, energy, and biological resources are successfully implemented and an ecologically sound, productive environment is maintained. The lives and livelihood of future generations depend on what the present generation is willing to do now.

LITERATURE CITED

Bartlett, A.A. 1998. An analysis of U.S. and world oil production patterns using Hubbert Curves. In press. *Journal of American Petroleum Geologists.*

Brown, L.R. 1995. *Who Will Feed China?* New York: W.W. Norton.

Campbell, C.J. 1997. *The Coming Oil Crisis.* New York: Multi-Science Publishing Company & Petroconsultants S.A.

Duncan, R.C. 1997. The world petroleum life-cycle: encircling the production peak. *Space Studies Institute* May 9: 1-8.

Duncan, R.C. and W. Youngquist. 1998. *Encircling the Peak of World Oil Production.* Issue # 2 Paper of the World Forecasting Program. 22 pp.

FAO. 1991. *Food Balance Sheets.* Rome: Food and Agriculture Organization of the United Nations.

Giampietro, M., and D. Pimentel. 1993. *The Tightening Conflict: Population, Energy Use, and the Ecology of Agriculture.* Edited by L. Grant. Negative Population Forum. Teaneck, NJ: Negative Population Growth, Inc.

Gleick, P.H. 1993. *Water in Crisis.* New York: Oxford University Press.

IFDC. 1998. *Global and Regional Data on Fertilizer Production and Consumption 1961/62-1995/96.* International Fertilizer Development Center, Muscle Shoals, Alabama: International Fertilizer Development Center.

Kendall, H.W., and D. Pimentel. 1994. Constraints on the expansion of the global food supply. *Ambio* 23: 198-205.

Kerr, R.A. 1998. The next oil crisis looms large–and perhaps close. *Science* 281 (21 August): 1128-1131.

Lal, R. and B.A. Stewart. 1990. *Soil Degradation.* New York: Springer-Verlag.

Myers, N. 1994. Tropical deforestation: rates and patterns. In *The Causes of Tropical Deforestation,* eds. K. Brown and D.W. Pearce. 27-41. Vancouver, British Columbia: UBC Press.

NAS. 1994. *Population Summit of the World's Scientific Academies.* Washington, DC: National Academy of Sciences Press.

Paoletti, M.G., and D. Pimentel. 1996. Genetic engineering in agriculture and the environment. *BioScience.* 46(9): 665-673.

Pimentel, D. and M. Pimentel. 1996. *Food, Energy and Society.* Niwet, CO: Colorado Press.

Pimentel, D., C. Harvey, P. Resosudarmo, K. Sinclair, D. Kurz, M.McNair, S. Crist, L. Sphpritz, L. Fitton, R. Saffouri, and R. Blair. 1995. Environmental and economic costs of soil erosion and conservation benefits. *Science* 267: 1117-1123.

Pimentel, D., J. Houser, E. Preiss, O. White, H. Fang, L. Mesnick, T. Barsky, S. Tariche, J. Schreck, and S. Alpert. 1997a. Water resources: agriculture, the environment, and society. *BioScience* 47(2): 97-106.

Pimentel, D., M. McNair, L. Buck, M. Pimentel, and J. Kamil. 1997b. The value of forests to world food security. *Human Ecology* 25(1): 91-120.

Pimentel, D., C. Wilson, C. McCullum, R. Huang, P. Dwen, J. Flack, Q. Tran, T. Saltman, and B. Cliff. 1997c. Economic and environmental benefits of biodiversity. *BioScience* 47(11): 747-757.

Pimentel, D., O. Bailey, P. Kim, E. Mullaney, J. Calabrese, F. Walman, F. Nelson, and X. Yao. 1998a. Will the limits of the Earth's resources control human populations? *Environment, Development and Sustainability* (in press).

Pimentel, D., M. Tort, L. D'Anna, A. Krawic, J. Berger, J. Rossman, F. Mugo, N. Doon, M. Shriberg, E.S. Howard, S. Lee, and J. Talbot. 1998b. Increasing disease incidence: environmental degradation and population growth. *BioScience* 48(10): 817-826.

Postel, S. 1996. *Last Oasis: Facing Water Scarcity.* New York: W.W. Norton and Co.

PRB. 1997. *World Population Data Sheet.* Washington, DC: Population Reference Bureau. Science. 1995. Cities as disease vectors. *Science* 270: 1125.

Sheridan, D. 1983. The Colorado–an engineering wonder without enough water. *Smithsonian* February 45-54.

Shetty, P.S. and N. Shetty. 1993. Parasitic infection and chronic energy deficiency in adults. *Supplement to Parasitology* 107: S159-S167.

U.S. Congressional Record. 1997. U.S. foreign oil consumption for the week ending October 3. *Congressional Record (Senate)* 143 (October 8): S10625.

USBC. 1996. *Statistical Abstract of the United States 1993.* Vol. 200th ed. Washington, DC: U.S. Bureau of the Census, U.S. Government Printing Office.

USDA. 1996. USDA Weekly Feedstuffs Report. *USDA Weekly Feedstuffs Report* 02 (25): 1-2. WHO. 1992. *Annual Statistics.* Geneva: World Health Organization.

WHO. 1996. *Micronutrient Malnutrition–Half of the World's Population Affected.* World Health Organization, 13 November 1996, 1996. Pages 1-4 No. 78.

WRI. 1992. *World Resources.* ed. World Resources Institute. New York: Oxford University Press.

WRI. 1994. *World Resources 1994-95.* Washington, DC: World Resources Institute.

Youngquist, W. 1997. *Geodestinies: The Inevitable Control of Earth Resources Over Nations and Individuals.* Portland, OR: National Book Company.

Avenues to Ecosystem Balance in a Human World

James D. Arney

SUMMARY. This paper presents the yield comparisons from a wide range of silvicultural regimes when applied to nineteen United States National Forests in the Pacific Northwest. The objective is to highlight the range of yield, value and biological parameters that result given any one of these regimes is followed over the next 100 years. Many non-forestry professionals are pressing for no harvest or selection-type all-aged forest harvesting regimes in the Pacific Northwest. The question is, that if these regimes do not provide comparable wood volumes to clear-cutting, the public continues to demand wood products, and the wildlife and plant biodiversity is permanently altered, "Is this where we want to go?". *[Article copies available for a fee from The Haworth Document Delivery Service: 1-800-342-9678. E-mail address: getinfo@haworthpressinc. com <Website: http://www.haworthpressinc.com>]*

KEYWORDS. Clearcutting, forest inventory, forest planning, forest yield, harvest planning, sustained yield

INTRODUCTION

Extending reserves for specific endangered species is a monocular view at least as destructive to humankind as an ever-expanding human population growth without regard to adequate food, shelter and quality

James D. Arney, 3486 SW Tegart Avenue, Gresham, OR 97080 USA.

[Haworth co-indexing entry note]: "Avenues to Ecosystem Balance in a Human World." Arney, James D. Co-published simultaneously in *Journal of Sustainable Forestry* (Food Products Press, an imprint of The Haworth Press, Inc.) Vol. 9, No. 1/2, 1999, pp. 45-57; and: *Contested Issues of Ecosystem Management* (ed: Piermaria Corona, and Boris Zeide) Food Products Press, an imprint of The Haworth Press, Inc., 1999, pp. 45-57. Single or multiple copies of this article are available for a fee from The Haworth Document Delivery Service [1-800-342-9678, 9:00 a.m. - 5:00 p.m. (EST). E-mail address: getinfo@haworthpressinc. com].

45

of life. Harvests from forests and fields are necessary to sustain the human population. To curtail these harvests for wildlife needs most certainly has an impact on the human species depending on these resources. The world is made up of finite resources. It can sustain only a finite population of species.

This paper describes the development of a two-level analytical model as a pilot trial. The objective is to develop an understanding of the relative impacts of varying goals on human, wildlife and ecosystem dynamics assuming limited geographic dispersion and resources. Oregon and Washington in the United States may be considered a macro level in this trial. Nineteen United States National Forests within these two States may be considered micro models at the second level. Sustained yields of forest products and services are simulated for 100-year periods from each micro model. The sustained yields of these forests are affected by the kind of silvicultural systems being applied in order to meet the demands for ecosystem management.

If the geographic extent of the macro model is constrained, then what human population dynamics can be sustained given the outputs from the forest models. The attempt here is to determine what balance is necessary between the human species and its environment within a specific geographic area. Drawing additional resources from outside the model would be depleting someone else's balance.

The objective of this paper is to draw attention to the quantifiable aspects of ecosystem management and what is already known about demands for and production of forest resources.

PACIFIC NORTHWEST NATIONAL FORESTS

Visualize the forests of the United States Pacific Northwest. These forests are made up of mostly intolerant species primarily including Douglas-fir (*Pseudotsuga menziesii*) and Ponderosa pine (*Pinus ponderosa*). Associated species include Western white pine (*Pinus monticola*), Noble fir (*Abies nobalis*), Western larch (*Larix occidentalis*) and Lodgepole pine (*Pinus contorta*).

As these stands advance in time without management or catastrophic events, such as fire or disease, they evolve into mixtures including Pacific silver fir (*Abies amabilis*), Grand fir (*Abies grandis*), White fir (*Abies concolor*) and Sitka spruce (*Picea sitchensis*). Moist coastal forests develop more tolerant mixtures including Western hemlock (*Tsuga heterophylla*) and Western red cedar (*Thuja plicata*).

Tolerance is judged largely by crown density, ability to clean the bole, and the ability of reproduction to take hold and develop under fairly dense crown canopies (Baker, 1950). Prior to the arrival of Europeans to America, native tribes and lightning provided frequent, light fires throughout the forests of the Northwest. As the tribes declined (due to European diseases and invasion) and the U.S. Forest Service developed the Smokey Bear anti-fire campaign (early 1900s), the forests have been allowed to evolve into more tolerant mixtures of species. For these reasons most forests of the Northwest are made of trees less than a few hundred years of age and still contain mostly intolerant species.

While there are many other plant and animal species that live and die in these forests, the mixtures and magnitudes of all species are dependent upon and determined by the primary tree species which characterize each forest. Therefore, the principal silvicultural regime that is chosen for management of these forests will determine the future for all plant and animal species that make up the nature of these forests of the Western United States.

The U.S. Forest Service has divided the public forests of the Northwest into nineteen National Forests averaging approximately 500,000 hectares (1,200,000 acres) each. The databases for these forest inventories were downloaded from the Internet and loaded into Microsoft Access databases. Each database contains the complete, actual tree records from permanent plots distributed systematically across each National Forest. Each cluster of plots were compiled to produce species, age, size, structure tables that now characterize the variety of stand composition and distribution within each National Forest. After setting aside roads, stream buffers (following State regulations by class of stream) and lands not capable of at least 12 meters (40 feet) of height in fifty years (Site Index 40-feet), we have approximately 4.7 million hectares (11.6 million acres) of productive, sustainable forest. These nineteen forest databases are the basis upon which the analyses and comparisons are drawn for this paper (see Table 1). They range from sea level to over 2,000 meters (6,000 feet) elevation and site productivity from 0 to 40 meters (130 feet) of height in fifty years. Productivity is inversely linear to elevation in this region. This fact increases in significance when we review the databases to find that

TABLE 1. First Decade Annual Harvest Volume Based on a 100-Year Planning Period.

National Forest	Gross Hectares	Net Hectares	Cubic Meters (×1000)			
			Clearcut	Seed Tree	Shelterwood	Selection
Colville	444,927	359,279	824	653	454	312
Deschutes	649,629	112,212	258	208	143	101
Fremont	449,844	27,803	47	45	29	18
Gifford Pinchot	555,218	428,022	1,929	1,592	1,147	837
Mt. Hood	371,252	293,137	1,378	1,087	784	571
Malheur	590,830	70,050	140	125	84	59
Ochoco	388,086	110,567	117	97	62	49
Okanogan	690,381	267,390	580	443	302	207
Olympic	255,888	195,535	936	759	564	405
Rogue	254,947	205,870	818	642	458	326
Siskiyou	442,819	356,128	1,311	1,067	765	548
Siuslaw	254,940	205,870	1,645	1,267	921	656
Mt. Baker-Snoqualmie	478,287	215,169	968	826	596	428
Umatilla	566,549	227,306	552	438	307	217
Umpqua	398,447	321,093	1,527	1,185	856	627
Wallowa-Whitman	994,072	225,377	521	420	288	205
Wenatchee	630,979	351,162	903	724	518	358
Willamette	678,000	533,976	2,944	2,311	1,661	1,216
Totals	**9,540,240**	**4,688,731**	**17,738**	**14,171**	**10,125**	**7,261**
% of Clearcut			**100%**	**80%**	**57%**	**41%**

current age class distributions reflect the impact of extensive, lower-elevation railroad logging in the early 1900s.

METHODS OF ANALYSIS

As each database was compiled to develop the species, age, size, density structure of each cluster of plots, a few other indices were also computed. These include a site productivity index (dominant height in fifty years) and a stand clumpiness index. The stand clumpiness is a measure of the uniformity of stocking among plots in each stand or cluster. Tree dimensions (diameter and height) provide the means to estimate an index to vertical distribution while among plot variation provide the means to estimate an index to horizontal distribution. Plots in an even-aged plantation will produce low clumpiness indices while plots in all-aged, mixed species natural stands will produce high clumpiness indices. Both of these indices were compiled and stored for each cluster of plots in every database.

Each of these nineteen forests then grew forward for 100 years with summaries produced at each decade (i.e., 2000, 2010, . . .2090) written back to each database. The Forest Projection System (FPS Version 5.1) (Arney, 1996-97) was used to project these stands because it contains:

- Most recent and complete calibration against observed permanent growth plots;
- Calibrated for over twenty tree species of the Northwest;
- Uses an Individual Tree, Distant Dependent model driven by Site and Clumpiness;
- Directly reads and writes to Microsoft Access databases;
- Has facility to reflect survival and growth impacts from site preparation, brush control, planting, thinning and fertilization as well as from variation in site productivity and stand clumpiness; and,
- Applies a common tree taper volume function so that all species and forests may be compared on a standard set of merchantability and valuation specifications.

Volumes for all species on all National Forests were computed using 0.3-meter (1-foot) stumps, 9.75-meter (32-foot) logs, 15-centimeter (6-inch) minimum log diameters, 20-centimeter (8-inch) minimum tree diameter at breast height and 5% deductions for hidden defect and breakage. Logs were valued by the following (US$/1000 board feet):

Species	6-inch logs	12-inch logs	16-inch logs
Douglas-fir	$500	$607	$775
Red cedar	525	585	700
Western hemlock	420	505	700
True firs	314	405	620
Hardwoods	314	405	405

Management costs included $185/ha ($75/acre) for site preparation, $457/ha ($185/acre) for planting, $185/ha ($75/acre) for brush control, $371/ha ($150/acre) for spacing and $12/ha/year ($5/acre/year) for overhead expenses. Logging costs were $170/Mbf (1000 board feet) for skidders, $200/Mbf for cable systems (over 40% slope) and $390/Mbf for helicopter (over 70% slope).

Four major silvicultural regimes were compared on each National Forest. These regimes are defined (Smith, 1962) and applied as follows:

Even-Aged Stand Development

Clearcut Regime–removal of the entire stand in one cutting with reproduction obtained artificially through planting of species and densities defined by Forest and elevation;

Seed Tree Regime–removal of the mature timber in one cutting, except for a small number of seed trees (10-20 per hectare or 4-8 per acre) left singly or in small groups with fill planting to supplement natural seed fall;

Shelterwood Regime–the removal of the mature timber in a series of cuttings, which extend over a relatively short portion of the rotation. This encourages the establishment of essentially even-aged reproduction under the partial shelter (40-80 per hectare or 16-32 per acre) of seed trees through natural seed fall.

Uneven-Aged Stand Development

Selection Regime–removal of the mature timber, usually the oldest or largest trees, either as single scattered individuals or in small groups at relatively short intervals (3-6 cuts per 100-years). These cuts are repeated indefinitely, by means of which the continuous establishment of reproduction is encouraged through natural seed fall and an uneven-aged stand is maintained.

In each of the Seed Tree and Shelterwood Regimes the residual seed trees were never included in the total harvested volumes because of the recent insistence from State and Federal wildlife staff that these trees should contribute to standing snags and down woody debris accumulations.

Plantations were stocked at 740 per hectare (300 trees per acre) on low site productivity (less than 24 m Site Index) and 860 per hectare (350 trees per acre) on all higher sites. Seed Tree Regimes were fill planted to these same densities where natural seed fall was inadequate. Preferred species for planting varied by National Forest and elevation zone are as follows:

National Forest	Low Zone	Elevation Limit (m)	High Zone
Colville	Douglas-fir		
Deschutes	Ponderosa pine	1500	Douglas-fir
Fremont	Ponderosa pine	1500	Douglas-fir
Gifford Pinchot	Douglas-fir	1200	Noble fir
Mt. Hood	Douglas-fir	1200	Noble fir
Malheur	Ponderosa pine	1500	Doublas-fir
Ochoco	Ponderosa pine	1500	Douglas-fir
Okanogan	Douglas-fir	1400	Noble fir
Olympic	Douglas-fir	900	Noble fir
Rogue	Douglas-fir	1500	Noble fir
Siskiyou	Douglas-fir		
Siuslaw	Douglas-fir		
Snoqualmie	Douglas-fir	900	Noble fir
Umatilla	Ponderosa pine	1200	Douglas-fir
Umpqua	Douglas-fir	1500	Silver fir
Wallowa-Whitman	Ponderosa pine	1200	Douglas-fir
Wenatchee	Douglas-fir	1400	Noble fir
Willamette	Douglas-fir	1200	Noble fir
Winema	Ponderosa pine	1500	Red fir

A 100-year planning period was used in order to evaluate the alternative regimes as influenced by at least a one-third turnover to 2nd rotation yields under the plantation and natural stand development of each regime. This results in a slight, but general, increase in sustainable yield levels as the forest comes under a continuous, full-stocking implementation. Clearcuts were limited to 48 hectares (120 acres); but the average stand size is closer to 10 hectares (25 acres) on these forests with some as small as one acre.

RESULTS

Table 1 shows the summaries from all nineteen individual forests in cubic meters and hectares. Table 2 displays the same information in

TABLE 2. Mean Annual Harvest Removals over a 100-Year Planning Period.

National Forest	Gross Acres	Net Acres	Scibner BdFt ($\times 1000$)			
			Clearcut	Seed Tree	Shelterwood	Selection
Colville	1,099,460	887,814	145,481	102,286	74,641	52,200
Deschutes	1,605,297	277,287	42,892	33,318	24,014	17,559
Fremont	1,111,610	68,703	8,488	6,607	4,668	3,440
Gifford Pinchot	1,372,000	1,057,684	331,043	268,297	196,656	146,410
Mt. Hood	917,402	724,372	229,847	179,638	130,658	95,748
Malheur	1,460,00	173,100	23,025	20,143	14,753	10,747
Ochoco	959,000	273,223	22,411	18,223	12,592	10,341
Okanogan	1,706,000	660,747	90,571	70,143	50,821	36,866
Olympic	632,324	483,187	164,678	132,418	100,013	72,002
Rogue	630,000	508,725	143,779	112,698	81,246	59,214
Siskiyou	1,094,250	880,029	237,786	187,846	136,633	100,871
Siuslaw	630,000	508,725	339,812	243,779	175,870	127,818
Mt. Baker-Snoqualmie	1,181,894	531,704	166,511	140,529	102,568	73,462
Umatilla	1,400,000	561,695	89,508	68,356	49,161	35,684
Umpqua	984,602	793,454	276,914	209,038	152,051	111,952
Wallowa-Whitman	2,456,451	556,928	83,801	64,910	46,839	33,825
Wenatchee	1,559,213	867,757	144,190	113,635	81,777	59,022
Willamette	1,675,407	1,319,508	535,274	404,747	293,550	214,968
Winema	1,099,999	451,681	57,402	45,683	32,484	22,862
Totals	23,574,909	11,586,323	3,133,413	2,422,294	1,760,995	1,284,991
% of Clearcut			100%	77%	56%	41%

Scribner board feet and acres. A potential sustainable forever, annual harvest of approximately 3 billion board feet will be reduced by 23% under seed tree regimes, 44% under shelterwood regimes, 59% under selection regimes and over 90% under current USFS practices.

Table 3 presents the accumulative net income from harvests in US dollars from each of the regimes. The potential sustainable forever, annual harvest income is approximately $1 billion per year. Moving to a selection-type forestry practice will reduce this by about 58 percent. Current USFS practices and policies have created a net negative cash flow into the US Forest Service rather than any outflow. County school district budgets based on net income from these lands are severely and permanently impacted by these new practices.

Table 4 provides some insight into the trends in major species composition after 100 years if each of these major silvicultural re-

TABLE 3. First Decade Annual Harvest Income Based on a 100-Year Planning Period.

National Forest	Gross Acres	Net Acres	US$ Values (× 1000)			
			Clearcut	Seed Tree	Shelterwood	Selection
Colville	1,099,460	887,814	31,828	25,032	17,399	12,445
Deschutes	1,605,297	277,287	19,213	15,263	10,661	7,766
Fremont	1,111,610	68,703	2,708	2,534	1,737	1,063
Gifford Pinchot	1,372,000	1,057,684	103,341	84,469	60,948	43,938
Mt. Hood	917,402	724,372	75,463	60,524	43,653	30,883
Malheur	1,460,000	173,100	5,564	4,970	3,351	2,348
Ochoco	959,000	273,223	5,182	4,403	2,952	2,526
Okanogan	1,706,000	660,747	20,094	15,808	10,672	8,008
Olympic	632,324	483,187	48,837	39,894	29,260	21,560
Rogue	630,000	508,725	51,848	41,697	30,403	22,689
Siskiyou	1,094,250	880,029	79,738	64,405	46,684	36,208
Siuslaw	630,000	508,725	132,064	103,084	74,269	59,191
Mt. Baker-Snoqualmie	1,181,894	531,704	45,696	39,182	28,348	18,990
Umatilla	1,400,000	561,695	22,092	17,719	12,446	8,763
Umpqua	984,602	793,454	102,529	79,941	57,769	41,063
Wallowa-Whitman	2,456,451	556,928	21,772	17,811	12,419	8,957
Wenatchee	1,559,213	867,757	39,001	31,845	22,738	16,054
Willamette	1,675,407	1,319,508	184,230	142,872	102,611	73,487
Winema	1,099,999	451,681	13,568	11,085	7,668	5,543
Totals	**23,574,909**	**11,586,323**	**$1,004,768**	**$802,538**	**$575,988**	**$421,482**
% of Clearcut			**100%**	**80%**	**57%**	**42%**

gimes is applied consistently throughout the period. It is quite obvious that moving to a selection-type regime for the intolerant species mixes of the Northwest will result in the end of the Douglas-fir and Ponderosa pine forests. Applying the selection-type thinning treatments will hasten this transition because the larger Douglas-fir and Ponderosa pine will be removed first to make the thinnings viable economically. Neither of these species will re-establish themselves under forest cover at these density levels. The resulting species will be hemlock, spruce, cedar and true fir. All non-tree species and wildlife species common to the Douglas-fir and Ponderosa pine forests will be impacted by this new selection forestry practice. Population densities of these other species will undergo changes to levels for forest types that have never existed in this region in recorded history. To change from

TABLE 4. Ending Major Species Composition Based on a 100-Year Planning Period.

National Forest	Gross Hectares	Net Hectares	Major Species			
			Clearcut	Seed Tree	Shelterwood	Selection
Colville	444,927	359,279	DF	DF/PP	DF/GF	GF/WH
Deschutes	649,629	112,212	PP/DF	PP/DF	DF/GF	GF/WH
Fremont	449,844	27,803	PP/SF	PP/SF	PP/SF	SF/PP
Gifford Pinchot	555,218	428,022	DF/NF	DF/SF	SF/DF	SF/WH
Mt. Hood	371,252	293,137	DF/NF	DF/SF	WH/DF	WH/SF
Malheur	590,830	70,050	PP/DF	PP/DF	DF/GF	DF/GF
Ochoco	388,086	110,567	PP/DF	PP/DF	DF/PP	DF/GF
Okanogan	690,381	267,390	DF/NF	DF/SF	DF/GF	GF/WH
Olympic	255,888	195,535	DF/NF	DF/WH	DF/WH	WH/RC
Rogue	254,947	205,870	DF/NF	DF/SF	SF/DF	SF/WH
Siskiyou	442,819	356,128	DF	DF/WH	DF/SF	SF/WH
Siuslaw	254,940	205,870	DF	DF/WH	DF/WH	WH/SS
Mt. Baker-Snoqualmie	478,287	215,169	DF/NF	DF/SF	DF/WH	WH/SF
Umatilla	566,549	227,306	PP/DF	DF/PP	DF/GF	GF/DF
Umpqua	398,447	321,093	DF/SF	DF/SF	DF/WH	WH/SF
Wallowa-Whitman	994,072	225,377	PP/DF	PP/DF	DF/GF	GF/DF
Wenatchee	630,979	351,162	DF/NF	DF/WH	DF/WH	WH/SF
Willamette	678,000	533,976	DF/NF	DF/WH	WH/DF	WH/SF
Winema	445,145	182,785	PP/RF	PP/SF	PP/SF	SF/WH
Totals	**9,540,240**	**4,688,731**				

clearcut regimes to selection regimes in the Northwest is making a huge change in future non-tree species, wildlife species, insect dynamics, disease potentials and wildfire intensity. Douglas-fir and Ponderosa pine exist here in abundance because they are volunteer species on open ground after fire, volcanoes and clearcuts. The natural (undisturbed) transition is to more tolerant species of hemlock and true fir; but, as observed in the forests that Lewis and Clark found in 1804-6, the major species were Douglas-fir and Ponderosa pine. This is because periodic catastrophic events (fire, weather, earthquakes) throughout Northwest history have resulted in these forests returning to Douglas-fir on a regular basis.

If we have learned anything from observing Northwest natural history, it is that these forests have repeatedly returned to the intolerant species of Douglas-fir and Ponderosa pine on a regular basis. If we chose not to emulate fire by applying small clearcuts throughout the forest, then nature will apply fire over large contiguous areas in its own harvest. We may not be pleased with the result. As is observed in these Tables, the tradeoff of moving away from Clearcut regimes in the U.S. Northwest toward Shelterwood and Selection regimes (Table 5) results in the following:

- Major impacts on long-term sustained yield of forest products (59% reduction)
- Major impacts on forest-provided School and Road revenues (58% reduction)
- Major impacts on tree species mixtures and associated wildlife (end of Douglas-fir)

CONCLUSIONS

Before we rush off in new directions with regard to managing existing intolerant-species forests, it would be worthy of our time and consideration to evaluate the consequences. In an effort to protect existing plant and animal species by a "kinder and gentler" forestry we may be causing more damage than good.

Using the results from the projection of these nineteen National

TABLE 5. Mean Annual Harvest Removals on the Gifford Pinchot National Forest.

Period	Scribner BdFt (×1000)			
	Clearcut	Seed Tree	Shelterwood	Selection
2000	314,218	259,908	187,126	138,936
2010	317,490	261,581	188,921	140,615
2020	320,445	263,870	191,586	142,674
2030	325,950	266,001	194,268	144,804
2040	330,024	269,194	196,986	145,381
2050	334,982	270,697	199,104	147,018
2060	335,117	271,261	201,351	149,739
2070	339,303	272,636	201,913	151,061
2080	337,368	273,373	202,626	151,604
2090	355,532	274,445	202,671	152,261
Average	331,043	268,297	196,655	146,409
	100%	81%	59%	44%

Forest inventories and a reasonable set of silvicultural specifications, it is quite clear that:

- These impacts of the new silviculture regimes are not generally understood
- Current decisions to do away with clearcutting will have long-term impacts
- These decisions will most likely do away with Douglas-fir as a major species
- Intolerant species forests will be replaced with tolerant species forests
- About $1 billion annual revenue is severely reduced or lost
- More analytical analyses and discussions of impacts are needed

One obvious conclusion is that the U.S. public will continue to use wood products. If these products are not produced locally, then from where will they come? Currently the United States uses about 50.7 billion board feet of wood each year. That is equal to about 208 board feet per person per year. On that basis, the population of Washington and Oregon (7,262,000 persons) demands about 1.5 billion board feet of wood each year. These forests have the capacity to produce about twice that quantity.

Using one-half of the wood products demand per person (100 bdft/yr) of the U.S., it is also obvious that Italy with a population of 57.5 million people requires another 5.7 billion board feet annually forever! Italy provides nearly none of its own wood requirements. Which forests from which country will supply these needs?

As Curtis (1998) summarized so well in a recent *Journal of Forestry* article, "*Conflicts often arise between political and social pressures, economics, and inherent biological limitations, and compromise is often needed, within the bounds of biological feasibility.*" (This author provided the underlining.) As forestry professionals, we must provide the details and range of impacts of making various policy decisions. So far much decision-making has gone on with limited or no analyses of impacts. We have sufficient documented history to know that this is not a logical path to follow. The following summary is taken from the textbook, *The Practice of Silviculture*, by David M. Smith:

No account of the selection method would be complete without mention of the half-forgotten attempt to apply the economic-selection method in the virgin forests of the Douglas-fir and associated species in the Northwest. This policy proved disastrous because partial cuttings in these ancient forests opened the way for accelerated deterioration of residual stands under the attacks of insects, fungi, and atmospheric agencies (Munger, 1950; Isaac, 1956). Furthermore, the method was unsuitable for the regeneration of Douglas-fir, which is less tolerant than its competitors in this particular region. The selection method is applicable to Douglas-fir only in dry situations where it grows as a physiographic climax in relatively open stands.

The failure of the selection method in West Coast Douglas-fir is an outstanding example of the difficulty of attempting to convert over-mature stands into productive units by selection cutting. (Smith, 1962, pp. 511-512)

LITERATURE CITED

Arney, James D. 1996-97. Calibration of the Forest Projection System for Western Oregon and Western Washington. Forest Biometrics Reports.

Baker, Fredrick S. 1950. Principles of Silviculture. McGraw-Hill Book Company. New York. 414pp.

Curtis, Robert O. 1998. "Selective Cutting" in Douglas-fir, History Revisited. Journal of Forestry. 96(7):40-46.

Isaac, L.A. 1956. Place of partial cutting in old-growth stands of the Douglas-fir region. USDA Forest Service. Pacific Northwest Forest and Range Experiment Station. Portland, Oregon. Research Paper No. 16.

Munger, Thorton T. 1950. A look into selective cutting in Douglas-fir. Journal of Forestry. 48(1):97-99.

Smith, David M. 1962. The Practice of Silviculture. 7th Edition. John Wiley & Sons, New York. 578pp.

Forest Management on a Natural Basis: The Fundamentals and Case Studies

Orazio Ciancio
Piermaria Corona
Francesco Iovino
Giuliano Menguzzato
Roberto Scotti

SUMMARY. Forest management has been conventionally based on two paradigms: (i) perpetuity of the forest based on the equilibrium between standing volume, standing volume increment and allowable cut; (ii) constrained optimisation of commodities (marketable or not). The latter, basically output-oriented, paradigm, has favoured simplifications of forest ecosystem structure and composition. The development of applied ecology has highlighted how dangerous such simplifications are for the ecosystems' functionality. In this perspective forest management on a natural basis is gaining growing recognition. Fundamental modifications of foresters' attitudes are required. Forest ecosys-

Orazio Ciancio is Professor of Forest Management and Piermaria Corona is Associate Professor of Forest Inventory, Istituto di Assestamento e Tecnologia Forestale, Università di Firenze, via San Bonaventura 13, 50145 Firenze, Italy.

Francesco Iovino is Associate Professor of Forest Ecology and Giuliano Menguzzato is Associate Professor of Forest Management, Dipartimento di Agrochimica e Agrobiologia, Università di Reggio Calabria, Piazza San Francesco di Sales 7, 89061 Gallina di Reggio Calabria, Italy.

Roberto Scotti is Research Assistant, Istituto di Assestamento e Tecnologia Forestale, Università di Firenze, via San Bonaventura 13, 50145 Firenze, Italy.

The work, carried out with equal contributions by the authors, was partially supported by funds from Università di Firenze (Fondi ex 60%).

[Haworth co-indexing entry note]: "Forest Management on a Natural Basis: The Fundamentals and Case Studies." Ciancio, Orazio et al. Co-published simultaneously in *Journal of Sustainable Forestry* (Food Products Press, an imprint of The Haworth Press, Inc.) Vol. 9, No. 1/2, 1999, pp. 59-72; and: *Contested Issues of Ecosystem Management* (ed: Piermaria Corona, and Boris Zeide) Food Products Press, an imprint of The Haworth Press, Inc., 1999, pp. 59-72. Single or multiple copies of this article are available for a fee from The Haworth Document Delivery Service [1-800-342-9678, 9:00 a.m. - 5:00 p.m. (EST). E-mail address: getinfo@haworthpressinc.com].

tems need to be perceived as entities with an intrinsic value and as complex, self-regulating, dynamically changing systems. A holistic and synthetic approach is required. Abandoning the strategy of forest normalisation, an adaptive management approach is needed to frame operational practices. This paper discusses: (i) the possible development of the theory of forest management on natural bases, and associated methodological fundamentals; (ii) the main guidelines for technical implementation of the proposed concepts; and (iii) case studies of Italian situations. *[Article copies available for a fee from The Haworth Document Delivery Service: 1-800-342-9678. E-mail address: getinfo@haworthpressinc. com <Website: http://www.haworthpressinc.com>]*

KEYWORDS. Forest ecosystems, forest management theory, systemic silviculture, sustainability, Italy

INTRODUCTION

Forest management has been conventionally based on two paradigms: (i) perpetuity of the forest based on the equilibrium between standing volume, standing volume increment and allowable cut; and (ii) constrained optimisation of commodities (marketable or not). The latter, basically output-oriented paradigm, has favoured simplifications of forest ecosystem structure and composition. The development of applied ecology has highlighted how dangerous such simplifications are for the ecosystems' functionality.

The fundamental contribution of classical theory to forest preservation and to the development of forestry should not be undervalued. Nonetheless we need to correctly identify its limits particularly concerning applications to forests as ecosystems. In the meantime the actual operational ability of the proposed methodological framework to yield better results must be proved.

Proceeding in this direction, this paper discusses (i) possible development of the theory of forest management on natural bases and associated methodological fundamentals, (ii) main guidelines for technical implementation of the proposed concepts, and (iii) case studies of Italian situations.

THE BASES FOR INTERPRETATION

Sylvicultural methods have traditionally been classified on the basis of the forest regeneration approach they implement. Well-recognised methods are hence the different types of clear-cutting systems, shelter-wood systems, selection systems and coppice treatments. On these bases, technical sylvicultural operations (the procedures) are perceived as the main focus of forestry (Larsen 1994), whereas, as we already mentioned, a fundamental modification to the approach is required, focusing directly on the forest as an ecosystem.

Fundamental biological principles apply to forest ecosystems as they do to all living beings. The search for functional efficiency (i.e., the system's own objective) becomes the fundamental objective of forest management. Acceptance of such a paradigm leads to forest management on a natural basis. In such a perspective:

- the forest is perceived as natural entity that has an intrinsic value;
- it is necessary to abandon the sylvicultural framework centred on the simplistic equilibrium between standing volume, standing volume increment and allowable cut;
- management practices are guided by an adaptive approach, based on trial and error, rather than on 'normalisation' schemes.

In principle, current sylvicultural practices aim at forest regeneration with a predefined model in mind. The aim is to develop 'regular' structures with normalised stocking, increment and age or diameter distribution, for even-aged and uneven-aged forests, respectively. In both cases, sylvicultural practices try to enforce a model as if forest ecosystems could be governed by controlling a few key variables and practically ignoring other aspects classifying them as casual effects. Yield tables, and the corresponding norm for uneven-aged forests, are the main expression of the idea that, in principle, by managing forests precisely following such optimal schemes, forest growth will probably match model expectation. This modelling approach has attained great credibility and has been extensively accepted also because, objective methods and evaluations could be implemented through mathematics, giving sylviculture, forest management and forest economy an aura of objectivity. However, it is quite often discouraging to match actual observations and the results of forest dynamics simulations. Like many complex biological systems, forests are characterised by unpredictable and undetermined reactions, multiple feedback links and close dependency on initial conditions (Scotti 1997; Corona and Scotti 1998).

On the application side, foresters in the field could feel more confident having scientific experimental evaluations as a technical basis. In practice, basic simplified schemes do not find direct application. In attempts at adapting the approach to actual ecological sustainability, basic schemes have been complicated but fundamental principles have not been abandoned: inherent forest heterogeneity has been reduced favouring homogeneity, its apparent disordered and chaotic structure has been forcibly ordered (Ciancio and Nocentini 1997a,b,c).

Sylviculture, as opposed to other non-sustainable forest exploitation practices, aims at preserving the internal organisation and feedback relations of forest ecosystems. Nonetheless, human intervention, artificial by definition, and impacting the structure of forest stands, provokes a certain level of stress in the system (Rogers 1996). Artificial impact needs to be constrained within the forests' limits of acceptability. Understanding that natural systems are able to preserve their internal organisation, withstanding even major structural modifications, could help find key elements in this issue. Shifting methodological focus from *a priori* determination to *a posteriori* evaluation or re-evaluation, requires a heuristic approach or a system theory of trial and error. Successive forest transformations resulting from human interventions, whether of structural or marginal nature, need to be observed and interpreted considering the complex interactive relations linking management subjects (the forest and man). Many decades of practical forest management have taught that the current deterministic approach, that expects to explain and govern the system, by managing a few key variables, could not succeed. It is necessary to recognise that even short-term predictions are not sufficiently reliable. Specifically, as far as natural forests are concerned, subjective and intuitive judgements play a substantial role in day-by-day choices, relying on monitoring to verify the effectiveness of the choices.

Building on such premises is it possible to define any forest management strategy with a minimum of operational detail? Probably the question should be reversed. If quantitative prediction of the behaviour of a complex biological system like a forest is not reliable, what was the meaning of the apparent operational detail available before such premises? Looking forward: forest planning and management strategy will be based on system auditing monitoring, inspecting ecosystem development, and through successive attempts, understanding forest resiliency and hence identifying proper limits for sylvicultural intervention.

TECHNICAL IMPLEMENTATION

To a certain extent, this perspective proposes a cultural revolution and it understandably provokes controversies at different levels in Europe (Portoghesi 1996). In reality, during the last fifteen years, different proposals moving in a common direction have appeared in the scientific literature. Among the many, five proposals appear as particularly relevant: (i) Ciancio introduced the 'modular cutting system' (Ciancio et al., 1982) that became the reference cultivation form of what was successively identified as systemic sylviculture (Ciancio and Nocentini 1997a); (ii) 'holistic forestry' which led to the development of the European foresters' 'Pro Silva' association (Mlinsek 1990); (iii) in quite different ecological conditions, a tropical forest in southern Africa, the holistic approach in biological sciences is considered vital for the conservation of such threatened ecosystems (Seydack 1995); (iv) the forest management approach related to 'disturbance ecology,' based on numerous studies of natural forest dynamics in relation to hazards of different nature, occurring at different geographic scales (Rogers 1996); and (v) 'ecosystem management' (Brooks and Grant 1992; Grumbine 1994) developed in north America from Franklin's New Forestry (Kohm and Franklin 1997), with the main objective of preserving and enhancing biodiversity.

The essential features common to these proposals could be summarised as follows:

- appreciation of the forest as a self-organising system pursuing global goals;
- adoption of reversible interventions (maximising future intervention options);
- adaptive management approach, proceeding by successive corrections;
- fundamental role of observation and interpretation of the transformations occurring, be they of marginal or structural nature, as complex system reactions to abiotic, biotic and anthropic factors.

Three methodological corollaries provide the background for the foregoing:

- the systematic nature of the analysis, considering all direct and indirect forest values (environmental, historical, cultural, experimental, didactic, recreational, landscape, etc.) together with reference to system structure and organisation (complexity, biodiversity, regeneration ability, etc.), over a range of ecologically relevant scales from both the spatial standpoint (from the tree group, to the stand, the forest, the landscape, etc.) and in time perspective (long-term stability, accounting for catastrophic events or climatic changes, etc.);

- globally focusing on the bi-directional relationships linking forest management subjects (the forest and man);
- emphasising the importance of ecosystem reactions and dynamic feedback consequent to human intervention.

The proposed management approach envisions specific suggestions for systems at different functional and efficiency levels, although the technical methods do not necessarily differ. It is, therefore, possible to define a general framework of technical guidelines for a wide range of intervention levels. Adjustments to the specific requirements of each level are implemented by modifying intervention parameter values (intensity, frequency, etc.) within the given framework (Jensen and Bourgcon 1994; Ciancio and Corona 1995; Ciancio et al. 1996; Corona et al. 1996; Colpi 1997; Ciancio et al. 1997). The following are the most relevant aspects of the general framework:

- identification of the specific values of each forest complex:

  - intrinsic values, belonging to the forest as such, currently related to naturalistic aspects
  - functional values, assigned to the forest by man

- interpretation of the forest as a functioning structure, where each unit is related to others and its state and dynamics are also influenced by external decisions and actions (open system);
- overcoming the sharp spatial distinction of management targets (absolute preservation on one side and intensive wood production on the other): preservation of complexity and biodiversity is a prominent requirement throughout the entire area;
- identification and evaluation of the negative impacts on the system due to human activities affecting specific values: felling, grazing, fires, tourism, etc. These activities normally affect tree stand composition, simplifying (eventually destroying) the somatic structure and age distribution. As a consequence, soil fertility, slope

stability, animal and plant biodiversity, plant health, aesthetic and recreational qualities, etc., are negatively affected too;
- preservation of system connectivity, reducing fragmentation to a minimum;
- search for impact-reducing cultivation methods that preserve existing values and promote others: temporary logging bans, extending rotation periods, reshaping of logging tracts, adoption of a modular cutting system, recovery of species mixture, releasing particularly large trees, regulation of grazing, etc. The disturbance engendered by sylvicultural intervention should not exceed the intensity and frequency of natural perturbations that, without undermining its reaction ability and allowing for the preservation of its intrinsic values, characterise the forest under consideration;
- superseding *a priori* yield determination and aiming instead at a planning approach that relies on monitoring of subsequent yield levels as the means of verification.

Sylvicultural treatment should emphasise the forest's intrinsic evolutionary dynamics, supporting natural self-organisation processes that occur in the stands. Depending on the specific conditions, support work may be quite limited (e.g., in the case of management oriented towards *sensu stricto* preservation) or it may be more active in the dynamics of biocenoses.

- The fundamental assumption is the lack of rigid schemes. Different specific objectives need to be adopted for each case, adapting to each particular environment. Instead of necessarily trying to converge on predetermined, so-called normal structures, interventions are based on detailed comparative evaluations of the effects of preceding actions.
- Active forest regeneration processes occurring under previous generation shelter are a fundamental reference for foresters' actions. Abandoning the idea of a rigid spatial distribution of forest structural characteristics offers the possibility of enhancing those processes as well as the forest's structural complexity favouring natural irregularities in the spatial and temporal distribution of regeneration.
- Tree felling criteria, in very general terms, are linked to growth conditions of single trees or tree groups. Interventions will

modify such conditions favouring and eventually completing natural selection due to the continuous evolution of the stands. The inherent risk in artificial interventions, of blind modification of the stands' genetic frequencies should be minimised, avoiding, for example, too early clearing of young stands and offering natural selection, at least in some instances, the opportunity of choosing the individuals most suited to become adult components of the system.

• Attention should be paid to minimising alterations in organic matter cycles; only removing what is truly important to remove, leaving dead tree, decomposing branches, etc.

CASE STUDIES OF ITALIAN SITUATIONS

Actual implementation of the proposed approach is illustrated in the following section with reference to specific Italian forests where the application of traditional sylvicultural approaches had to some extent failed to achieve the goal of establishing an equilibrium. Examples are very weak demonstrations, since opposing examples are always relatively easy to point out. Nevertheless there is a need to state that operational works are in progress in order to couple theory with practice.

The first case concerns the Italian stone pine (*Pinus pinea* L.) forest of Alberese (Grosseto, Tuscany, Central Italy). Forests of this species were traditionally cultivated mainly for edible seed production. Regeneration was fundamentally achieved through plantations for the purpose of developing even-aged single storied structures, obviously with a relevant impact on ecological cycles and conditions. The characteristic quasi uneven-aged structures of spontaneous stone pine forests throughout the Mediterranean basin have practically been ignored. The Alberese forest was particularly suited to set up an experimental research plan on finding practical alternatives to traditional systems, since what would be called 'irregular' structures are quite common there.

The second case concerns the Turkey oak (*Quercus cerris* L.) and Italian oak (*Q. frainetto Tenn.*) forests at Macchia Grande di Manziana near Rome (Central Italy). Stand structures here are extremely variable and relevant regeneration problems occur even when what is regarded as the reference sylvicultural treatment is applied. Following the proposed approach, the research is trying to evidence that the state of dynamic equilibrium is not necessarily linked to ordered structures.

The third one concerns a forest of Brognaturo (Cosenza, Calabria, Southern Italy) characterised by stands where silver fir (*Abies alba Mill.*) and common beech (*Fagus sylvatica* L.) are present with different degrees of mixture. This mixture was once much more frequent along the Apennine Range. Forest exploitation over the past centuries severely reduced fir diffusion as well as the richness, stability and productivity of the forests. To recover forest quality very site specific practices must be developed.

Beyond their specific peculiarities, the considered cases, especially the first two, are examples of a very common condition of Italian high-forests, at least in the central and southern parts of the country. As practising foresters know well, for most forests, it is quite confusing to try to assign them a 'normal' structure: they generally are far from being so intensively cared for to approach an uneven-aged model and yet reluctant to be ordered in a regular even-aged fashion. Exploitation, wild fires, and uncontrolled grazing intensively modified the stands. Forest ecosystem reactions generated structures that, according to Hellrigl (1986), would be better classified as 'composite' rather than irregular, avoiding the de-qualifying sense inherent in the latter term.

Alberese stone pine forest–The Alberese stone pine forest, which is in the regional park of Uccellina, covers 445 hectares, extending along the Tyhrrenean coast, from the north facing slopes of the Uccellina mountain range to the Ombrone river. It is an alluvial undulating lowland area, where ground water occasionally emerges at lower levels. The climate is mesothermic, between sub-humid and sub-arid. Potential vegetation is of the *Quercetum ilicis* type, characterised by evergreen sclerophyllous species. The forest was artificially established, starting in the XIX century, to halt shifting of coastal dunes and to protect the coastal agricultural area from sea winds.

During the last decades, forest management was mainly concerned with edible stone pine seed production: eliminating older and less productive individuals, pruning productive subjects, and clearing the maquis to favour seed collection and eventually regeneration growth. Stand structures here are generally more complex than in other stone pine forests cultivated for seed production. For this reason experimental plots have been established here to study stand dynamics, particularly regeneration dynamics, and to evaluate the possibility of achieving better bio-ecological stability on natural basis: favouring regeneration while seed exploitation continues (Ciancio et al. 1986, 1996).

The following structural types have been identified through field observations and data analysis: young single-storied, two-storied small groups, multi-storied groups of different size, full-size single-storied. The shapes and dimensions of groups show direct relationships with the gaps where they originated. Single groups occupy from 100-200 m^2 to 400-500 m^2, and even larger than one hectare in some instances. Natural regeneration is concentrated in two- and multi-storied groups, particularly in even-aged ones with basal area below 16 m^2/ha. Seedlings are favoured by local water availability. Their development is limited due to wildlife plundering the seed and grazing.

The Alberese stone pine forest, which originated as even-aged stands, has progressively loosed that ordered structure as natural regeneration began to take over, and also because of seed collection. Having established a protected area, the process was greatly reduced. Ongoing experimental sylvicultural treatments aim at reactivating the regeneration processes implementing a preservative procedure fulfilling the landscape requirements of a nature conservation park. Small gaps are created where maquis species are controlled to stimulate seed development while 20 percent of the cones are left behind, unharvested, older trees are gradually removed, seed-producing trees are pruned to increase yield. As it is now organised, sylvicultural interventions will take place on the same site after 6-8 years.

Macchia Grande di Manziana oak forests–The oak forests of Macchia Grande di Manziana extend over 540 hectares, in a flat area west of Bracciano lake. Here we are in the cold subzone of Pavari's *Lauretum* class, on fertile soils that originate from volcanic deposits. These woods have significant historic, cultural and environmental value: they are among the very few remnants of the forests that originally characterised the vast area including the Sabatini, Ceriti and Tolfa mountains. Forest exploitation here, dates back to Etruscan times, however, since the XIII century have been alternatively ruled by two opposing institutions: 'Pio Istituto di Santo Spirito' (a religious institution) and the current owner, 'Università Agraria di Manziana' (the current body, which is a public lay institution). The main product has been and still is fuelwood, mainly for the local community.

Having been exploited mainly following commercial criteria, the forest's current structures are extremely variable and serious regeneration problems are occurring. The studies (Agrimi et al. 1991; Ciancio 1991) identified four main structural types and evidenced that natural regeneration preferentially occurs in openings between 300 and 700 m^2, depending on the structural type (Agrimi et al. 1991; Ciancio 1991).

The uniform shelterwood system is considered the optimal sylvicultural treatment for these oak high-forests in Italy (de Philippis 1955), but even-aged treatments like this have frequently produced unsatisfactory results. The approach under observation aims at preserving the forest's structural complexity, gradually controlling species composition, stimulating oak regeneration by seed clearing small openings between 250 and 350 m^2, gradually thinning the stands as they grow and maintaining other species such as *Acer campestre* L. and *Ostrya carpinifolia Scop.* through coppicing. Similar to Huffel's (1919) 'futaie claire,' forest structure becomes multi-storied, with small overtopping groups having each different ages, shapes and dimensions. Yield is determined exclusively on the basis of sylvicultural needs, taking care not to exceed natural growth, which is generally quite low: 0.15 percent. Treatments results are monitored in 5 years cycles at the compartment level and every 10 years at the forest level.

Brognaturo fir-beech forests–The Brognaturo forests are located on the northern mountains of Calabria called 'le Serre.' They cover over 600 hectares at elevations ranging from 950 to 1050 m a.s.l., on fertile forest soils, where climatic conditions fall in the Castanetum and warm Fagetum classes of Pavari's classification. Originally the forests where characterised by fir and beech mixtures with pronounced abundance of the first. Fir presence has been dramatically reduced by irrational exploitation and the forest structure has been severely modified by excessive grazing. The actual problem is to try to recover a natural state of equilibrium.

The forest has been analysed from the sylvicultural and growth perspective (Ciancio and Menguzzato 1979), identifying and mapping the main categories on the basis of species composition, structure, age, crown cover and regeneration status. Today, fir presence is down to 31 percent, on the average. Mixtures occur mainly by groups that can be very large. Mixed groups appear as single-storied, even-aged structures with fir in dominant positions and beech as the co-dominant species. Two distinct stories appear at lower crown coverage levels. Regeneration is absolutely absent at high coverage levels while it appears where stands have been thinned or the first shelterwood felling has been performed.

In such environments, fir regeneration and development is hindered by uniform treatments over large areas. Light and frequent interventions are required in order to favour seed dispersal and gradually free existing regeneration. Frequent interventions are required also in the beech groups, favouring the reintroduction of the firs. It makes little sense to determine and apply any fixed rotation length. Highest priority is given to forest structural development, requiring very stand-specific interventions (Iovino and Menguzzato 1997).

CONCLUDING REMARKS

In a world-wide perspective, the conventional bases for forest management have undergone significant revisions. Born as timber production management, sylviculture inherited agricultural ideas and approaches, and has gradually attempted to shift towards applied ecology. Yet the influence of the traditional approach on proposed revisions has to be fully recognised.

In particular, in central and southern Italy forest management has come to stake in the last decades. The foresters' knowledge and wisdom remain unexpressed to a great extent because the forest management proposal is worn out. 'Normalisation,' proposed as the guiding scheme, has become a barrier, especially from external perception point of view.

Sylviculture on a natural basis implies a profound modification in approach. Forest ecosystems, as complex self-organising living organisms, have an intrinsic value, before and above the values man attributes them (Corona and Portoghesi 1997). Forest management is implemented on an adaptive basis, by a limited impact trial and error approach, developing as a complex relationship.

Technical specifications are not necessarily new. The foresters' wisdom and experience are essential guides in the effort to understand the specific requirements of each stand. Monitoring and detailed analysis provide the basis for technical verification.

The case studies presented here offer examples of common conditions where the foresters' ability to intervene is practically under-exploited if 'normalisation' schemes were to be pursued. The foresters' freedom and responsibility to operate in a manner that favours the forest's capacity for self-organisation offer much greater chances of success.

LITERATURE CITED

Agrimi, M.G., Ciancio, O., Portoghesi, L. and R. Pozzoli. 1991. I querceti di cerro e farnetto di Macchia Grande di Manziana: strttura, trattamento e gestione. Cellulosa e Carta 42(5):25-49.

Brooks, D.J. and G.E. Grant. 1992. New perspectives in forest management: background, science issues, and research agenda. Research Paper PNW-RP-456, USDA Forest Service, Portland.

Ciancio, O. 1991. La gestione dei querceti di Macchia Grande di Manziana: la teoria del sistema modulare. Cellulosa e Carta 42(1):31-34.

Ciancio, O. and G. Menguzzato. 1979. Indirizzi generali e di massima per il riordino colturale e la valorizzazione del bosco di Brognaturo. Annali Istituto Sperimentale per la Selvicoltura 10:79-136.

Ciancio, O., Mercurio, R. and S. Nocentini. 1982. Le specie forestali esotiche nella selvicoltura italiana. Annali Istituto Sperimentale per la Selvicoltura 12/13, 731 pp.

Ciancio, O., Cutini, A., Mercurio, R. and A. Veracini. 1986. Sulla struttura della pineta di pino domestico di Alberese. Annali Istituto Sperimentale per la Selvicoltura 17:169-236.

Ciancio, O. and P. Corona. 1995. La pianificazione dei sistemi forestali: applicazioni e prospettive. Atti, La progettazione ambientale nei sistemi agroforestali, IAED, Roma, pp. 22-37.

Ciancio, O. and S. Nocentini. 1997a. The forest and man: the evolution of forestry thought from modern humanism to the culture of complexity. Systemic sylviculture and management on natural bases. In: pp. 21-114. Ciancio O. (ed.), The forest and man, Accademia Italiana di Scienze Forestali, Firenze.

Ciancio, O. and S. Nocentini. 1997b. Forest management between ecology, economic and ethics. In: pp. 223-236. Ciancio O. (ed.), The forest and man, Accademia Italiana di Scienze Forestali, Firenze.

Ciancio, O. and S. Nocentini. 1997c. The scientific paradigm, "good silviculture" and the wisdom of the forester. In: pp. 257-268. Ciancio O. (ed.), The forest and man, Accademia Italiana di Scienze Forestali, Firenze.

Ciancio, O., Garfi V. and S. Nocentini. 1996. La pinede de pin pignon d'Alberese: une methode sylvicole nouvelle. Istituto di Assestamento e Tecnologia Forestale, Università di Firenze, Firenze (unpublished), 5 pp.

Ciancio, O., Corona, P. and S. Nocentini. 1998. Pianificazione e gestione dei boschi privati. EM Linea Ecologica 1 (fasc. sep.): XVI-XX.

Colpi, C. 1997. What kind of silviculture? In: pp. 197-209. O. Ciancio (ed.), The forest and man, Accademia Italiana di Scienze Forestali, Firenze.

Corona, P. and L. Portoghesi. 1997. Notes on ethics in silviculture. In: pp. 183-195. Ciancio O. (ed.), The forest and man, Accademia Italiana di Scienze Forestali, Firenze.

Corona, P., Iovino, F. and S. Lucci. 1996. La gestione dei sistemi forestali nella conservazione del suolo. Linea Ecologica 3:2-10, 4:4-15.

Corona, P. and R. Scotti. 1998. Forest growth-and-yield models: questioning support for sustainable forest management. Journal of Sustainable Forestry 7(3/4):131-143.

De Philippis, A. 1955. I querceti a foglia caduca. Atti del Congresso Nazionale di Selvicoltura, Firenze, pp. 133-151.

Grumbine, E.R. 1994. What is ecosystem management? Conservation Biology 8:27-38.

Hellrigl, B. 1986. La compartimentazione assortimentale. In: pp. 221-301. Nuove metodologie nella elaborazione dei piani di assestamento dei boschi. Isea, Bologna.

Huffel, G. 1919. Economie Forestière. Tome II, Paris.

Iovino, F. and G. Menguzzato. 1997. A return to complex formations through forest management. In: 211-221 pp. O. Ciancio (ed.), The forest and man, Accademia Italiana di Scienze Forestali, Firenze.

Jensen, M.E. and P.S. Bourgeon (eds.). 1994. Volume II: Ecosystem management: principles and applications. General Technical Report PNW-GTR-318, Portland, USDA Forest Service.

Kohm, K.A. and J.F. Franklin. 1997. Creating a forestry for the 21st century. The science of ecosystem management. Island Press, USA.

Larsen, D.R. 1994. Adaptable stand dynamics model integrating site-specific growth for innovative silvicultural prescriptions. Forest Ecology and Management 69:245-257.

Mlinsek, D. 1990. The future of forest management based on research results from virgin forest. Proceedings, XIX IUFRO World Congress, vol. 1, pp. 107-115.

Portoghesi, L. 1996. Un importante dibattito scientifico internazionale sulla questione forestale: ideologia o nuovo paradigma scientifico? L'Italia Forestale e Montana 5:355-363.

Rogers, P. 1996. Disturbance ecology and forest management: a review of the literature. USDA Forest Service, General Technical Report INT-GTR-336, 16 pp.

Scotti, R. 1997. Forest management amid determinism and indeterminism. In: pp. 151-158. Ciancio O. (ed.), The forest and man, Accademia Italiana di Scienze Forestali, Firenze.

Seydack, A.H.W. 1995. An unconventional approach to timber yield regulation for multi-aged, multispecies forests. I. Fundamental considerations. Forest Ecology and Management 77:139-153.

Biodiversity, Genetic Diversity, and Protected Areas in Turkmenistan

Habibulla I. Atamuradov
Galina N. Fet
Victor Fet
Raul Valdez
William R. Feldman

SUMMARY. The information is presented on the independent state of Turkmenistan as a rich depository of unique biodiversity. Biodiversity in Turkmenistan is well-studied compared to many adjacent areas due to the unique historical and political circumstances. The long and complicated geological history of Turkmenistan has provided a diverse arena for the formation of local biodiversity and endemism of fauna and flora. Diverse mountain vegetation of the Kopetdagh Range—a depository of plant genetic diversity—is characterized in detail. Endangered species of large mammals (many in the IUCN Red Data Book) are

Habibulla I. Atamuradov is Deputy Minister in the Ministry of Nature Use and Environmental Protection, Azadi 81, Ashgabat, 744000, Republic of Turkmenistan.

Galina N. Fet is Adjunct Assistant Professor of Biology in the Department of Biological Sciences, Marshall University, Huntington, WV 25755 USA.

Victor Fet is Associate Professor of Biology in the Department of Biological Sciences, Marshall University, Huntington, WV 25755 USA.

Raul Valdez is Professor of Wildlife Science in the Department of Fishery and Wildlife, New Mexico State University, Las Cruces, NM 88003 USA.

William R. Feldman is Director of Boyce Thompson Arboretum, Superior, AZ 85273 USA.

[Haworth co-indexing entry note]: "Biodiversity, Genetic Diversity, and Protected Areas in Turkmenistan." Atamuradov, Habibulla I. et al. Co-published simultaneously in *Journal of Sustainable Forestry* (Food Products Press, an imprint of The Haworth Press, Inc.) Vol. 9, No. 1/2, 1999, pp. 73-88; and: *Contested Issues of Ecosystem Management* (ed: Piermaria Corona, and Boris Zeide) Food Products Press, an imprint of The Haworth Press, Inc., 1999, pp. 73-88. Single or multiple copies of this article are available for a fee from The Haworth Document Delivery Service [1-800-342-9678, 9:00 a.m. - 5:00 p.m. (EST). E-mail address: getinfo@haworthpressinc.com].

73

listed and their current status is outlined. Suggestions are made for conservation of biodiversity in Turkmenistan. *[Article copies available for a fee from The Haworth Document Delivery Service: 1-800-342-9678. E-mail address: getinfo@haworthpressinc.com <Website: http://www.haworthpressinc.com>]*

KEYWORDS. Turkmenistan, biodiversity, Kopetdagh, vegetation, desert

We present information on the independent state of Turkmenistan as a rich depository of unique biodiversity. Turkmenistan (a Soviet Union republic before 1991) occupies 488,100 sq km. It is bordered on the west by the Caspian Sea, on the south by Iran and Afghanistan, on the north by Kazakhstan, and on the east and north by Uzbekistan. It is in the Asian temperate desert zone and has an annual precipitation of < 150 mm over most of the country, except the mountains of Kopetdagh and Kugitang.

100 YEARS OF NATURAL HISTORY IN TURKMENISTAN

Biodiversity in Turkmenistan is well-studied compared to many adjacent lands due to the unique historical and political circumstances. Culturally, Turkmenistan belongs to the Turkic-speaking part of the Islamic world. As part of the famous "Great Game" between the Russian and British Empires in Central Asia, Turkmenistan was the last colonial prize of the Russian tsars; its delineation from Afghanistan was completed only in the 1890s. A stunning rate of technological and cultural progress in this desert land of nomads was achieved in less than 30 years of imperial Russian rule. Since the 1880s, naturalists have attempted to describe the rich and peculiar flora and fauna of the magnificent sand deserts of Turkmenistan.

Early notes described the rich natural resources in deserts and mountains as well as the severe deforestation. Logging of juniper in the mountains, pistachio trees in the foothills, and saksaul shrubs in sand desert began as early as in the Neolithic Age, when early farming settlements emerged in the foothills of Kopetdagh. It continued through the era of the ancient Parthian Empire, whose capital, Nisa, now lies in ruins a few miles from Ashgabat, the capital of Turkmenistan. Timber was used in construction, as firewood, and also as a charcoal supply for smelting of metals. Green and populous oases, with such centers of culture and education as Khwarazm (Khiva), thrived in the Transcaspia in the times of the magnificent empires of Alexander the Great and his followers, only to be destroyed in the next millennium by Genghis Khan, Tamerlane, and other warriors. Human-influenced desertification expanded in these times; extensive grazing of sheep and camels by Huns and, later, Turkic tribes, contributed to soil deflation and erosion by desert winds and rare, but intensive rains.

The Transcaspian Region was immediately recognized as an important area for scientific studies. The world-famous Repetek Sand Desert Station was established in 1912 to study the geology of the Karakum sand desert. Biological stations and museums followed; the first extensive collections were made from the 1890s through the first decade of the twentieth century for major Russian natural history museums in Moscow, St. Petersburg, and Tiflis.

With the establishment of the Soviet regime after 1917, Russian science was artficially severed from European scientific thought. Original, mandatorily isolated Russian schools of theory in ecology and biogeography developed in the 1920s and 1930s. Primary data for this development flowed from many geographical areas of the Soviet Union, including Central Asia; the deserts and mountains of Turkmenistan continued to be an important site of basic field research.

Limited in their abilities to travel abroad, Soviet scientists traveled to exotic, "colonial" domestic places. As a result, the rich faunas of Turkmenistan is rather well known as compared to many adjacent areas. The well-known volumes of the "Fauna of the USSR" and even the more comprehensive "Flora of the USSR," published since the 1930s, were important landmarks, similar to the work of British naturalists in India.

There is a considerable expertise currently available on biodiversity of Turkmenistan. In the early 1990s, an international project was launched to document the known data on biodiversity of this region which led to a publication, in English, of the volume titled Biogeography and Ecology of Turkmenistan (V. Fet and K. Atamuradov, eds., 1994, Kluwer Academic Publishers, 680 pp.). This monograph embraced all areas of physical geography, ecology, botany, zoology and biogeography and was authored by 30 authors from Turkmenistan, Russia, Ukraine, and the USA. This book was the first comprehensive ecological monograph published in English about former Soviet republics of Central Asia.

While basic science in the Central Asian republics rather gained from the Russian "colonial" influence, natural resources, in contrast, were severely damaged by the Soviet way of handling the economy and social issues. Severe environmental problems have been inherited by the now independent Turkmenistan. In order to approach a solution to these problems, scientists and officials in the republic need the close attention and help of the international scientific community.

BIOGEOGRAPHY AND ENDEMISM

The long and complicated geological history of Turkmenistan has provided a diverse arena for the formation of local biodiversity. Specificity of fauna and flora of Kopetdagh is expressed in its mixed character: it includes a combination of western (mostly Mediterranean) and eastern (Turanian) elements, as well as local authochthonous endemics, usually at the species level.

In Turkmenistan, mountains and desert are divided only by a narrow (10 to 20 km) belt of the arid foothills. The biogeographic border between the Mediterranean-type mountains of Kopetdagh and the lowland continental desert of Karakum is one of the best expressed ecological and biogeographic boundaries that exists on the Earth. Over its geological history, Kopetdagh could have served as a biogeographic corridor for spider dispersal. In the Late Oligocene-Miocene (25 to 10 million years ago), reduction of the ancient Tethys Sea revealed an island/peninsular chain from the modern Balkans to the Armeno-Iranian Plateau. This chain was a natural corridor for dispersal, as many island chains are today (e.g., the Antilles or Sunda Islands). With aridization continuing from the Eocene through the Oligocene, landscapes gradually changed. By the Miocene-Pliocene (from 5 to 2 million years ago), the mountain uplift and receding Tethys Sea aridization separated deserts of Central Asia from those of Sind, the Middle East, and North Africa and promoted the vicariant speciation on desert lowlands. However, the mountain chains of Zagroz, Elburz, and Kopetdagh still could have served as effective dispersal routes. The sublatitudinal position of this uplifting mountain chain suggests that migrations of animals through it eastward or westward was not limited by latitudinal climatic changes (a common problem in such well-known dispersal cases as, for example, North/South American exchange). Moreover, the altitudinal zonation in mountains allowed dispersal of ecologically different animals migrating within specific mountain belts. Located between northern and southern deserts of Asia, these mountains could house mesophile fauna which could not survive aridization of adjacent lowlands.

In the Pleistocene (less than one million years ago), the Iranian mountain corridor undoubtedly was a site of constant dispersal and, probably, also of local speciation. Many local endemic species probably are of this age, especially plant species (Kamelin 1970). Transgressions of the Proto-Caspian Sea periodically returned these desert mountains to the island condition. During the recent glaciation (16,000 to 10,000 years ago) this corridor could have been invaded by almost modern European and Asian "refugee" species. Then, a new aridization disrupted many ranges and effectively isolated European forest and meadow species in mountain valleys such as the Aidere Valley in Southwest Kopetdagh. Flora and fauna in walnut and elm forests of this magnificent (ca. 30 km long) gorge bears strong European mesophile features.

Below, we give a concise, original (Fet 1994) review of the diverse vegetation in the Kopetdagh Mountains in order to illustrate diversity of ecosystems in Turkmenistan.

ECOSYSTEM DIVERSITY:
THE MOUNTAIN VEGETATION

Flora of Kopetdagh (1,942 vascular plant species) is believed to have originated from the Ancient Mediterranean stock common for all floras of Central Asia; its unusually high specific endemism (up to 18%; Kamelin 1970) reflects its prolonged isolation in the Neogene from all other mountains of Central Asia, especially those eastward of Kopetdagh. Arid woodlands (shiblyak) were formed in the lower belts by the early-middle Pliocene, and were impoverished later. In the Pliocene/Pleistocene time, the Kopetdagh Range was an important center of origin of mountain xerophyte flora; the mountain steppe communities in Kopetdagh were also formed by the early Pleistocene. The mountain steppe communities (in the middle and upper mountain belts) played important role in the autochthonous evolution of endemic species. In general, different age and origin of flora and vegetation of Southwest Kopetdagh determined existence here of extremely diverse set of plant communities. Currently, these communities are profoundly affected by human activity which leads to the rapid degradation of vegetation and desertification of the landscapes.

Our study of vegetation of Southwest Kopetdagh (the region of approximately 30,000 km^2) has been conducted from 1978 to 1986 in the Syunt-Khasardagh Natural Reserve (area ca. 300 km^2) and adjacent areas; it resulted in description of plant communitites on 602 plots, with 585 species of higher plants and 14 species of mosses registered. Key plot areas were mapped in the scale of 1:1,000 to 1:5,000 which will allow creation of the complex map of vegetation for this region. Maps of vegetation (1: 100,000) were compiled for 23,000 ha.

Semishrub (sagebrush) deserts. Sagebrush communities (*Artemisia herbaalbae* species group *A. badhysi, A. turcomanica,* and *A. kulbadica*) occupy most of the area of the foothills of Southwest Kopetdagh (300 to 800 m). Most widespread are communities dominated by *Artemisia* spp., *Poa bulbosa,* and desert sedge (*Carex pachystylis*); coverage of *Artemisia* spp. may reach from 5 to 40%; *Poa bulbosa,* from 5 to 20%, and *Carex pachystylis,* from 5 to 10%. These communities include numerous ephemerous and ephemeroid plant species. High degree of soil erosion due to cattle grazing leads to the common presence of petrophytes. Under heavy grazing, sagebrush coverage drops to 5-10%, and plant communities include such annual grasses as *Eremopyrum orientalis, Anisantha tectorum, Avena barbata,* and *Bromus japonicus.* In the Sumbar river valley and its tributaries, on the soils with high salt content, are found communities of *Artemisia olivieriana* and such halophytes as *Salsola dendroides, S. gemmascens,* and *Aellenia subaphylla.*

Semisavanna includes communities dominated by a perennial grass *Elytrigia trichophora* (coverage from 50 to 60%). Common codominants at 800 to 1,000 m include *Poa bulbosa, Helianthemum salicifolium, Convolvulus subhirsutus, Phlomis kopetdaghensis,* and *Perovskia abrotanoides* (an indicator of a disturbed habitat). Complexes of *E. trichophora* with *Festica valesiaca* spread up to 1,600-1,700 m and include characteristic species of meadows and steppes: *Galium verum, Crucianella sinenisii, Thymus trancsaspicus, Bunium longipes.*

Meadows are formed primarily by *Elytrigia repens* (coverage 20 to 80%) and are located from 700-800 to 1,500-1,600 m in the depressions of mountain plateaus, or in the river valleys. Other dominants are *Trisetum flavescens, Dactylis glomerata, Alliaria alliacea, Nepeta sintenisii, Crucianela sintenisii, Anisantha sterilis, Galium verum,* and *G. aparine.* Derived communities are dominated by *Hordeum murinum* and *Eruca sativa.*

Steppe vegetation is developed on mountain plateaus and are similar to the zonal steppes of Asia; dominant grasses here include *Stipa* spp. and *Festuca valesiaca.* The most common are communities of *F. valesiaca* on plateaus from 1,200 to 1,900 m. Common codominant plant species include *Stipa turcomanica, S. hohenackeriana, Galium verum, Thymus transcaspicus, Elytrigia trichophora,* and some species of shrubs.

Shiblyak (Mediterranean short-tree woodland). It is usually dominated by the Turkmen maple (*Acer tucomanicum*) and the Christ's thorn (*Paliurus spinachristi*). The Turkmen maple is a small tree or shrub, two to three meters tall; it is widespread from 800 to 2,500 m. Maple-shrub communities may cover from 20 to 80%; codominant shrubs are *Cerasus microcarpa, Ephedra intermedia, E. equisetina, Cotoneaster nummularia, Colutea gracilis, Paliurus spinachristii, Lonicera bracteolaris, Celtis caucasica, Jasminum fruticans,* and *Amygdalus communis.* The lower layer covers 10-20 to 80-90%, with such herbaceous dominants as *Anisantha sterilis, Trisetum flavescens, Fritillaria raddeanum, Allium paradoxum, Orthurus heterocarpus, Lamium turkestanicum.* When disturbed by logging and grazing, maple stands are more sparse, and herbaceous cover incorporates derived communities dominated by *Elytigia trichophora, Anisantha tectorum, Taeniatherium ornitum,* and *Poa bulbosa.* Complexes of maple and phryganoid (*Thymus transcaspicus* and *Perovskia abrotanoides*) communities are not uncommon. Maple forests in Southwest Kopetdagh are heavily disturbed by uncontrolled logging and grazing of sheep and goats.

The upper altitudinal limit of maple forest is 1,400 to 1,500 m; from below, maple forest is bordered by communities of the Christ's thorn (*Paliurus spinachristi*), a shrub which dominates plant communities from 300-400 to 700-800 m of altitude. The lower layer is comprised of smaller shrubs such as *Cerasus microcarpa, Colutea gracilis, Jasminum fruticans, Rubia florida, Rhamnus sintenisii,* and *Amygdalus scoparia.*

The shiblyak communities of Southwest Kopetdagh house high

number of fruit trees, shrubs, and vines valuable for selection, including pomegranate (*Punica granatum*), wild grapes (*Vitis sylvestris, V. vinifera*), fig (*Ficus carica*), wild apple (*Malus turkmenorum*), wild pear (*Pyrus boisiieri*), wild cherries (*Cerasus microcarpa, C. erythrocarpa, C. blinovskii*), wild prune (*Prunus divaricata*), almonds (*Amygdalus communis* and *A. scoparia*), and hawthorns (*Crataegus* spp.). Some of these species have been intensively studied.

Phryganoid vegetation, or tomillares. This Mediterranean type of vegetation is represented in Southwest Kopetdagh by the communities of small, fragrant semishrubs belonging to the family Lamiaceae including *Perovskia abrotanoides, Thymus transcaspicus*, and *Ziziphora clinopodioides*. Phryganoid communities are fragmentarily found from 1,000 to 1,500 m and form complexes with the vegetation of semisavanna and steppe.

Juniper woodland. Stands of *Juniperus turkomanica* with 30 to 40% coverage can be found only in the easternmost part of the region. Within the Syunt-Khasardagh Reserve, we found fragments of well-developed juniper stands only on well-moistened slopes at 1,300 to 1,600 m. Most of the area in these sites is covered by complexes of juniper and maple with mesophile grass and herbaceous species in lower layer. Single juniper trees may be found at altitudes as low as 200 or 300 m in the shiblyak or petrophyte communities.

Tragacanthoid vegetation (mountain xerophytes) in Kopetdagh is limited primarily to the representatives of the genera *Acanthophyllum, Acantholimon*, and *Tragacantha*. In Southwest Kopetdagh, these species are found in the middle and upper mountain belts at the altitudes above 1,500-1,600 m in complexes with steppes and juniper woodland.

Deciduous forest. Well-developed forest communities formed by tall trees such as elm (*Ulmus carpinifolia*), walnut (*Juglans regia*), Syrian ash (*Fraxinus syriaca*), and *Thelycrania meyeri*, are found primarily along the narrow mountain river valleys with high humidity. Walnut and ash forests are found exclusively in the valleys, whereas elm communities can be seen also on the mountain plateaus and slopes where they exist due to the higher precipitation, provided particularly by winter snow and spring rainfall.

Walnut riparian forest is confined to a very narrow (50 to 100 m wide) strip along the mountain rivers at the altitudes from 1,000 to 1,500 m. *Juglans regia* is accompanied by *Fraxinus syriaca, Thely-*

crania meyeri, Prunus divaricata, Lonicera floribunda, Rubus sangui-noides, and *Rosa lacerans.* The mesophile herbaceous layer inlcudes *Anisantha sterilis, Elytrigia repens, Cousinia umbrosa, Anthriscus lon-girostris, Physocaulis nodosus,* and *Allium paradoxum.* Common hygrophile vegetation includes *Equisetum ramosissimum* and *Mentha longifolia.* Total area ocupied by walnut forests of Southwest Kopetdagh does not exceed 80 ha. In such highly humid ash and walnut communities we found a number of rare or endemic species of orchids (such as *Ophrys transhyrcana* and *Epipactis veratrifolia*) and ferns (such as *Ophioglossum vulgatum*).

A magnificent, relict Eastern sycamore, or plane tree (*Platanus orientalis*), included in the Red Data Book of the former USSR, forms complexes with ash and walnut forests and meadow and hygrophyle vegetation along large valleys. The major population of plane tree in the Aidere valley included 204 trees older than 20 year age growing in a very narrow strip, up to 1,100 m. Preservation of this unique population depends entirely on anti-erosion efforts which should prevent mudslide formation in the watershed slopes and plateaus.

Desert riparian forest, or tugai. Fragmentary tugais occupy very narrow strip (10 to 30, rarely 50 to 100 m wide) along the Sumbar Valley at the altitudes from 200 to 700-800 m. Almost entire area occupied by tugais in the past is now transformed into fields, gardens, and settlements. Communities which may be considered close to original tugai, are formed by such characteristic trees as the *Populus euphratica*) and, rarely, *Salix persa* and *Elaeagnus orientalis,* but especially by salt-tolerant *Tamarix florida* and *T. meyeri.* Tall mesophile grasses such as *Imperata cylindrica, Arundo donax,* and *Erianthus ravennae* form complexes with hygrophile communities. Communities dominated exclusively by a giant reed *Arundo donax* is found from 400 to 1,000 m next to surfacing groundwater on mountain slopes and in the valleys; this original grass is widely used by local population for construction. *Tamarix* forms communities with annual grasses and halophyte vegetation. Tugai communities are heavily modified due to the constant changes in riverbed and in groundwater level as well as erosion, uncontrolled ploughing, cattle grazing, and logging.

Hygrophile vegetation is widespread in the region along the rivers and springs in the foothills and lower mountian belt and is represented commonly by the reed (*Phragmites communis*) and also by sedges

(*Carex diluta*, *C. divisa*, and *C. polyphylla*), *Juncus gerardii*, *Heleocharis uniglumis*, and hygrophile moss and even liverwort species. Variants of hygrophile communities are formed depending on water supply, and swamped areas can be often found locally.

Mountains and foothills of Turkmenistan still house rich gene pool of plants and animals. Sustainable development of local ecosystems depends on preservation of their key components. The key species should be targeted as genetic diversity objects for study and sustainable development under various regimes of protection.

ENDANGERED MAMMALS AND PROTECTED AREAS

A number of endangered species of large mammals are still preserved and can be preserved within the protected territories of Turkmenistan.

Among the 101 vertebrate species listed in the Red Data Book of Turkmenistan (1985), are 27 mammals, 35 birds, 30 reptiles, one amphibian, and eight fishes. Turkmenistan is inhabited by about one-third of the animal species listed in the Red Data Book of the former USSR; more than 11% of those species are found, within the territory of the former USSR, only in Turkmenistan. Means of effective conservation of rare species are discussed, including their protection in eight Natural Reserves (*zapovedniki*) of the Republic of Turkmenistan.

Many wildlife species occuring in reserves have been extirpated in (largely arid) areas outside of reserves. Protected areas provide opportunities for applied research for developing strategies of preservation of genetic diversity (e.g., for large ungulate mammals) and for strategies that utilize wild and domestic species (sheep, cattle) in multispecies grazing systems. The degraded rangelands outside of reserves are in urgent need of grazing strategies that halt declining range conditions. Wild species of grazing mammals (onagers, urials, mountain goats, gazelles) that have evolved in utilizing arid rangelands with minimal detrimental impacts offer an alternative to the use of exotic domestic species.

Below, we give a brief review of the rare and endangered species of large mammals (including those from the IUCN Red Data Book) which inhabit (or recently inhabited) Turkmenistan.

LEOPARD (*Panthera pardus tullianus*) was widespread in mountains and foothills of Turkmenistan in the late 19th and early 20th centuries. Throughout Turkmenistan, 360 leopards were killed from 1924 to 1966. The population of Kopetdagh leopards is steadily declining. Its records are constant but sporadic in Kopetdagh. With the establishment of the Kopetdagh Reserve in 1976, and the Syunt-Khasardagh Reserve in 1979, regular observations of leopards were done in the 1980s in Central and West Kopetdagh. The total number of leopards in Turkmenistan probably does not exceed 30 to 40 animals.

ASIAN CHEETAH (*Acinonyx jubatus raddei*). Before World War II, there were about 40 cheetahs in Turkmenistan (Sludsky 1973); from 1930 to 1957 in Badghyz, 25 animals were shot or captured, and about 70 encounters recorded. Cheetahs were often found in Badghyz and Karabil until the late 1950s. Some still inhabited Northwest Turkmenistan during the 1960s and early 1970s. Today the cheetah can be considered extinct in Turkmenistan; even though some non-confirmed records indicate that single cheetahs still are present in the Northwest, the existence of a viable population there is doubtful. Reintroduction of this unique large predator to the Badghyz and Kaplankyr Reserves is recommended from Iran.

TURANIAN TIGER (*Panthera tigris virgata*). Tiger lived in Kopetdagh (the Atrek, Sumbar, and Chandyr Valleys) as well as in valleys of the Amudarya, Murghab, and Tedzhen, but it was almost completely exterminated in the first decades of the 20th century. The last tiger in the Sumbar Valley was killed in January 1954 (this specimen is on display in the Ashgabat City Museum). Tigers entering from Iran were recorded until the early 1960s. Unfortunately, this subspecies is now probably extinct from the world fauna.

WILD SHEEP, or URIAL (*Ovis orientalis arkal*). Turkmenistan has a large surviving population of wild sheep (ca. 7,000 animals). Local sheep belong to a moufloniform species with 58 chromosomes (Valdez 1982). Most of this population lives in the arid mountains and foothills within two Natural Reserves: Badghyz (3,000 to 3,500 animals) and Kopetdagh (2,000 to 2,500 animals). Human activity has significantly decreased the population of the mountain sheep in Turkmenistan. The most critical points are fragmentation of populations and competition with domestic animals. Water availability, especially in the semidesert plateau of Badghyz, is scarce. The most important measures should include: construction of additional artificial water sources, cleanup of natural springs and reintroduction into areas where urials have been extirpated.

HEPTNERS MARKHOR (Capra falconeri heptneri). This mountain goat was recently surveyed by one of the authors (R. V.; Weinberg et al. 1997). The subspecies is found only on the western slopes of the Kugitang range. The recent census estimated number of *C. falconeri* within Turkmenistan as 227 animals; within the entire range of this species in Central Asia, there are not more than 1,000 goats. This species is protected in the Kugitang Reserve.

BEARDED GOAT (Capra aegagrus turkmenicus). It is found in Maly and Bolshoi Balkhan ranges and in Kopetdagh. Its numbers have decreased dramatically in the last decades. Most of the population is concentrated in Central Kopetdagh, where about 2,000 goats are found within the borders of the Kop etdagh Reserve. The Bolshoi Balkhan population is also declining. This mountain range was especially rich in goats in the past (they were found even in the foothills, at 100-200 m above sea level). The total number of bearded goats in Turkmenistan probably does not exceed 2,000. This species is protected in the Kopetdagh and Syunt-Khasardagh Reserves.

GOITER GAZELLE (Gazella subgutturosa). From the mid-19th century up to the 1930s, many researchers recorded herds of thousands of these gazelles. In the early 1940s the population of gazelles in Turkmenistan was estimated as more than 100,000 animals. Today, its range has decreased more than 70%; this gazelle is now.found only in isolated herds. Hunting of gazelles has been banned since 1950; however, this ban has not been effectively enforced, and extensive poaching continues. The only place where gazelles are relatively secure is the Badghyz Reserve, where its population reaches 3,000 to 4,000 animals; the total population in Turkmenistan today is estimated as not more than 5,000 or 6,000. Gazelles were introduced on Ogurchinsky Island in the Caspian Sea; their herd had more than 400 by the mid-1990s.

ONAGER, or KULAN (Equus hemionus onager). The Turkmen subspecies is currently found only in South Turkmenistan between the Tedzhen and Kushka Rivers. Onagers were recently introduced to the submontane plain of Central Kopetdagh and to the Kaplankyr Reserve (northern Turkmenistan).

In the 19th century, thousands of onagers lived in Turkmenistan. By 1935, only about 500 animals were left, all of them in Badghyz. Their number continued to decrease until the Badghyz Reserve was established in 1941, when only 250 onagers were left. In 1969, the Badghyz herd comprised 800 animals and in 1976, 1,254. Today, the Badghyz Reserve has about 7,300 onagers. This population increased to the point where it is damaging habitats in the Reserve and Croplands outside of it; its activity during the last five years led to the rapid desertification of the Reserve habitats.

Among other rare and endangered mammals protected in Turkmenistan are: bear (*Ursus arctos syriacus*) (not a resident species which occasionally visits from Iran); Bokhara deer (*Cervus elaphus bactrianus*); marbled polecat (*Vormela peregusna koshevnikovi*); otter (*Lutra lutra seistanica*); wild cats–karakal (*Felis caracal michaelis*), lynx (*F. lynx isabellina*) and manul (*F. manul ferrugineus*); and a number of species of bats and rodents.

PLANT GENETIC RESOURCES: VAVILOV'S LEGACY

An oustanding depository of plant genetic diversity in Turkmenistan is the Turkmen Experimental Station of Plant Genetic Resources (TES PGR) was created by the initiative of N. I. Vavilov in 1930 in the Southwest Kopetdagh (Garrygala). It is currently in critical condition. After the collapse of the USSR (1991) the Station is administered by the Turkmen Ministry of Agriculture. For the two last years the Station was not financed at all. Of the professionals who worked under VIR system, only two people are left. Compared to other VIR Stations, the TES was a specialized station, the southernmost and one of the smallest. Its collections of gene pool of 17 fruit cultures include 4,353 varieties; since the collapse of the USSR, some loss of the collection plants did happen. Still, the TES contains the largest in the world collection of pomegranate varieties (*Punica granatum*), large collections of local wild varieties and cultivars of fig, grapes, apple, pear, apricot, almond, walnut, pistachio.

The TES is located in the area of rich biotic conditions, with high number of endemics, high biodiversity (including useful plant species) and a very high diversity of wild fruit trees. The region has features of the arid subtropical climate: average year temperature 16.1°C; average January temperature 3.6°C; average July temperature 28.7°C; absolute minimum, − 19.8°C; absolute maximum, 48.0°C; length of the frostless period, 236 days; annual precipitation, 328 mm. Altitude of the TES varies from 312 to 550 m above sea level. Total area belonging to the Station is 734.3 ha, with old gardens on 43.8 ha, and young gardens on 17.3 ha.

The area surrounding the TES is characterized by an extensive agriculture; an excess of the labor force (part of which migrates to the cities); shortage of water for irrigation; and low fertility of garden and field plants. The current trend is decrease of the garden areas and an increase in grain and vegetable production. The style of administration largely remains the same as under the Soviet system (top-to-bottom decision-making, passivity, corruption, lack of responsibility, low professional skills, etc.).

The danger of physical loss of the collection samples is accompanied by the potential loss of identity or identifiability of germplasm. This is why backup work of the Station's core collections has been initiated. To sustain the Station's activity requires external support and funding which is possible only with foreign-based sponsorship. It would be also advisable to publish, in English, a volume of Station's research results so that international scientific community will become familiar with the Station's work.

The main goal at this moment is to preserve Vavilov's heritage–a genetic resource collection which can be used in future within the Central Asian region and for the gene banks throughout the world.

THE FUTURE

Turkmenistan joined the Biodiversity Convention in 1996. Currently, protected areas (*zapovedniki*) in Turkmenistan (total number eight, area 819,000 ha, or 1.7% of the country's territory) are islands of ecological diversity, especially in the mountains of Kopetdagh and Kugitang, and foothill plateau of Badghyz.

Further directions in the study and conservation of Turkmenistan biodiversity should continue surveying and monitoring of endangered species and protected territories. Maintaining contacts with the world research community becomes a necessary part of this process. The current dismal financial situation of the protected territories and genetic resources depositories (such as TES PGR) will be improved by cooperation with world conservation organizations which may take shape of joint grant proposals, field expeditions and projects, etc. Contacts can be established with Turkmenistan researchers and conservationists as well as with government officials responsible for the conservation of biodiversity.

Ecotourism might be one way for Turkmenistan to finance the conservation of its natural protected areas, so vulnerable under the continuing aridization. Ecotourist facilities, as well as joint scientific environmental projects, can be based in the eight existing Natural Reserves (Krasnovodsk, Kaplankyr, Syunt-Khasardagh, Kopetdagh, Badghyz, Repetek, Amudarya, and Kugitang) which represent all major landscapes of the republic. In the past, these reserves have traditionally played the role of biological field stations, hosting dozens of field researchers each year. The Turkmenistan Department of Natural Resources and Conservation is committed to furthering scientific studies directed toward the preservation of biodiversity, and welcomes joint surveys and sharing of technology by the interested foreign specialists and agencies. Today, it is important to maintain the existing high level of the academic research and long-term monitoring.

It is our common desire to see the human population of Turkmenistan living in balance with its diverse nature, and the state of Turkmenistan being peaceful and prosperous.

LITERATURE CITED

Babaev, A. G. et al. (Eds). Red Data Book of the Turkmen SSR, Vol. 1. Ashkhabad (in Russian and Turkmenian). 413 pp.

Fet, G. N. 1994. Vegetation of the Southwest Kopetdagh. PP. 149-172 In: Fet, V. and K. I. Atamuradov (Eds). Biogeography and Ecology of Turkmenistan. Kluwer Academic Publ., Dordrecht.

Fet, V., and K. I. Atamuradov (Eds). 1994. Biogeography and Ecology of Turkmenistan. Kluwer Academic Publishers, Dordrecht, The Netherlands. 650 pp.

Kamelin, R. V. 1970. Botanical-geographical features of the flora of the Soviet portion of Kopetdagh. Botanichesky zhurnal, 55(10) : 1451-1463 (in Russian).

Kamelin, R. V. (Ed.) 1990. Pistachio in Badghyz. Nauka, Leningrad, 231 pp. (in Russian).

Kucheruk, V. V. (Ed.). 1995. Mammals of Turkmenistan. Vol. 1: Carnivores. Ylym, Ashgabat, 309 pp. (in Russian).

Rustamov, A. K., and O. Sopyev. 1994. Vertebrates in the Red Data Book of Turkmenistan. PP. 205-229 In: Fet, V. and K. I. Atamuradov (Eds). Biogeography and Ecology of Turkmenistan. Kluwer Academic Publ., Dordrecht.

Shammakov, S. 1981. Reptiles of the lowland Turkmenistan. Ylym, Ashkhabad, 309 pp. (in Russian).

Valdez, R. 1982. The Wild Sheep of the World. Wild Sheep and Goat International, Mesilla, New Mexico. 186 pp.

Valdez, R., C. F. Nadler, and T. D. Bunch. 1978. Evolution of wild sheep in Iran. Evolution, 32: 56-72.

Weinberg, P., R. Valdez, and A. K. Fedosenko. 1997. Status of the Heptner's markhor (*Capra falconeri heptneri*) in Turkmenistan. Journal of Mammalogy, 78(3):826-829.

Longleaf Pine Ecosystem Restoration: The Role of Fire

James P. Barnett

SUMMARY. Longleaf pine (*Pinus palustris* Mill.) ecosystems once occupied over 36 million hectares in the southeastern United States' lower coastal plain. These fire-dependent ecosystems dominated a wide range of coastal plain sites, including dry uplands and low, wet flatlands. Today, less than 1.3 million hectares remain, but these ecosystems represent significant components of the Region's cultural heritage, ecological diversity, timber resources, and present essential habitat for many animal and plant communities. Fire was an essential component of the original longleaf pine ecosystems. The landscapes were characterized by open stands of mature longleaf pine with a savanna-like understory that were biologically diverse. Recent improvements in the technology to artificially regenerate longleaf pine has stimulated interest in restoring longleaf pine on many sites. Long-term studies show that the frequent use of fire hastens initiation of height growth, reduces undesirable competing vegetation, and stimulates growth and development of the rich understory. So, fire is an important element in establishing the species and is critical to achieve and maintain the biologically diverse understory that is characteristic of the ecosystem. *[Article copies available for a fee from The Haworth Document Delivery Service: 1-800-342-9678. E-mail address: getinfo@ haworthpressinc.com <Website: http://www.haworthpressinc.com>]*

KEYWORDS. *Pinus palustris*, biological diversity, fire-dependent ecosystems, reforestation, stand management

---

James P. Barnett, Southern Research Station, USDA Forest Service, Pineville, LA 71360 USA.

[Haworth co-indexing entry note]: "Longleaf Pine Ecosystem Restoration: The Role of Fire." Barnett, James P. Co-published simultaneously in *Journal of Sustainable Forestry* (Food Products Press, an imprint of The Haworth Press, Inc.) Vol. 9, No. 1/2, 1999, pp. 89-96; and: *Contested Issues of Ecosystem Management* (ed: Piermaria Corona, and Boris Zeide) Food Products Press, an imprint of The Haworth Press, Inc., 1999, pp. 89-96. Single or multiple copies of this article are available for a fee from The Haworth Document Delivery Service [1-800-342-9678, 9:00 a.m. - 5:00 p.m. (EST). E-mail address: getinfo@haworthpressinc. com].

INTRODUCTION

Currently there is considerable discussion about restoring ecosystems to some previous condition, but there seems little consensus on the means to achieve restoration; what are the target landscapes; what methodologies should be used; and how is success measured? The present condition of available sites, and legacies from the past land use, along with available technology and methods constrain restoration goals. Restoration of the longleaf pine (*Pinus palustris* Mill.) ecosystem in the southern United States is now receiving a great deal of attention (Landers et al. 1995, Noss 1989). The use of fire plays an important role in the restoration of this fire-dependent system.

Longleaf pine ecosystems once occupied over 36 million hectares in the southeastern United States' lower coastal plain from southern Virginia to central Florida and west to eastern Texas (Frost 1993). These fire-dependent ecosystems dominated a wide array of sites within the region. Today, less than 1.3 million hectares remain (Kelly and Bechtold 1990), with much of this in an unhealthy state. Longleaf ecosystems represent significant components of the Region's cultural heritage, ecological diversity, timber resources, and present essential habitat for many animal and plant communities. This once extensive ecosystem has nearly vanished. The objectives of this paper are to describe the longleaf pine ecosystem and its ecological and economic values, and explore possibilities for restoring the longleaf pine ecosystem to an important part of the southern forests.

THE LONGLEAF PINE ECOSYSTEM

The natural range of the longleaf pine covers most of the Atlantic and Gulf Coastal Plains with extensions into the Piedmont and mountains of north Alabama and northwest Georgia. The species occurs on a wide variety of sites, from wet, poorly drained flatwoods near the coast to dry, rocky mountain ridges (Boyer 1990). It is a long-lived tree, potentially reaching an age of several hundred years; but, longleaf pine forests are often exposed to catastrophic hazards such as tropical storms or fire and to continuing attrition from lightning which shorten possible rotation ages (Landers et al. 1995).

Longleaf pine is a very intolerant pioneer species and the seedlings go through a stemless grass stage. If competition is severe, they may remain in this grass stage for years. The ecosystem is distinguished by open, park-like "pine barrens," which are composed of even-aged and multi-aged mosaics of forests, woodlands, and savannas, with a diverse groundcover dominated by bunch grasses and usually free of understory hardwoods and brush (Landers et al. 1995). The diversity of understory plants per unit of area places longleaf pine ecosystems among the most species-rich plant communities outside the tropics (Peet and Allard 1993). Although the pine barrens are known for persistence and diversity, they occur on infertile soils. The ecological persistence of these areas is a product of long-term interactions among climate, fire, and traits of the key plants.

THE HISTORICAL ROLE OF FIRE

Fire was an essential component of the original longleaf pine ecosystems. Longleaf pine and bunch grass (e.g., wiregrass and certain bluestems) possess traits that facilitate the ignition and spread of fire during the humid growing seasons (Landers 1991). Frequent fire was largely responsible for the competitive success of longleaf pine and the grasses. These keystone species exhibit pronounced fire tolerance, longevity, and nutrient-water retention that reinforce their dominance and restrict the scale of vegetation change following disturbance. Fires that were ignited by Native Americans or that resulted from thunderstorms with frequent lightning prevailed over the region, a complex of quick-drying sites that are exposed to natural and anthropogenic disturbances. Many of these fires occurred during the growing season and largely prevented species native to other habitats from encroaching into the pine barrens. The chronic fire regime also maintained the soil structure and nutrient dynamics to which longleaf pine is adapted (McKee 1982). These fire effects tended to make longleaf pine sites more favorable to resident species than those indigenous to more nutrient-rich habitats.

DECLINE OF THE LONGLEAF ECOSYSTEM

The depletion of the longleaf ecosystem resulted from its many desirable attributes that have caused it to be exploited since the settlement of the nation by Europeans (Croker 1979). However, it was the event railroad harvesting in the late 1800's and early 1900's that provided assess to and depleted the vast remaining longleaf timberland. Cutting proceeded from the Atlantic states west through the Gulf Coast Region with increasing intensity of use with time. Longleaf pine logging reached a peak in 1907, when an estimated 74 million cubic meters were cut (Wahlenberg 1946). The longleaf pine ecosystem now occupies only a small part (less than 5 percent) of its original area. This habitat reduction is the reason for the precarious state of at least 191 taxa of vascular plants (Hardin and White 1989, Walker 1993) and key wildlife species such as the red-cockaded woodpecker, gopher tortoise, and southern fox squirrel (Landers et al. 1995).

Regeneration of longleaf pine was limited because of a combination of circumstances. The completeness of the harvest left little seed source for natural regeneration and much of the harvested land was cleared for cropland or pasture. Longleaf pine does not successfully invade open land in competition with more aggressive pine or grass species. Regeneration sometimes succeeded old-growth when periodic fires provided a seedbed and controlled woody competition, and when wild hogs did not reach a density high enough to destroy established seedlings (Landers et al. 1995). The disruption of natural fire regimes, resulting in part from forest fire protection policies implemented during the 1920s, allowed invasion of longleaf sites by hardwoods and more aggressive pine species. Longleaf pine and its associated species cannot compete under these conditions. Regeneration, both naturally and artificially, is more difficult than for any other southern pine due to the delay in stem elongation (the grass stage) that is a genetic trait of the species. Also, survival of planted bareroot nursery stock is generally poor and established seedlings in the grass stage are very sensitive to competition.

RESTORATION OF THE LONGLEAF PINE ECOSYSTEM

A key to restoration of the longleaf pine ecosystem is to ensure that its recovery benefits society. Without economic benefits, long-term conservation projects usually do not succeed (Oliver 1992). Longleaf pine forests have high economic value due to the quality of solid-wood products produced. Harvesting or forest management need not be eliminated or even moderately restricted to restore and maintain longleaf pine ecosystems, as evidenced by the fact that logging at the

turn of the century apparently had little effect on groundcover diversity (Noss 1989). Restrictions on harvest would be a disincentive to
many landowners and could result in the elimination of much of the
remaining longleaf pine on private lands.

Restoration of the longleaf pine ecosystem is achievable since
pockets of longleaf pine occur in much of its former range. It should
be feasible to gradually expand longleaf pine acreage through education, research, and commitment on the part of resource managers.
Restoration is now a goal on much of the public land in the southern
United States, where longleaf pine remains as a component of the
forest. In fact, much of the current acreage of the ecosystem occurs on
public lands.

A number of interacting factors will determine whether the restoration of the longleaf pine ecosystem can be achieved. These include the
capability to successfully regenerate longleaf pine on its native sites,
to use fire to enhance establishment and management of both the
overstory and the understory species, to educate the public and resource mangers on the value and technology of restoration, and to
evaluate restoration success.

Reforestation Technology. Utilization of the trees in the original
forest was so complete that inadequate numbers of seed trees remained
to naturally regenerate many of the harvested stands. So, artificial
regeneration must be used to restore longleaf on the appropriate sites
were it originally grew. Until recently, regeneration success from
planting was generally unacceptable due to problems related to severe
competing vegetation, delayed stem elongation, and poor storability of
bareroot seedlings. We now have the knowledge and technology to
reestablish longleaf pine by planting bareroot stock. The keys to successful establishment are: well-prepared, competition-free sites; healthy, top-
quality, fresh planting stock; meticulous care of stock from lifting to
planting; precision planting; and proper post-planting care (Barnett
1992). Attention must be given to all of these factors to obtain acceptable regeneration.

Planting of container stock is now accepted as the most successful
method of regenerating longleaf pine (Barnett and McGilvray 1997).
This improved survival and growth is generally attributed to root
systems that remain intact during lifting while the roots of bareroot
plants are severely damaged. Thus, container seedlings experience a
significantly shorter period of transplant stock or adjustment than

bareroot stock. However, using container stock does not eliminate the critical need for controlling competition during the first growing season after planting.

Role of Fire. Fire is an essential component of the restoration and management of the longleaf pine ecosystem. Long-term studies show that the frequent use of fire hastens initiation of height growth, reduces undesirable competing vegetation, and stimulates growth and development of species that are an essential component of the understory. Seasonal burning studies show that late spring burns are much more effective in the restoration process than the typical winter burns that are usually favored for other pine species (Grelan 1978). Fire is an important element in establishing the species and is a critical component for achieving and maintaining the biologically diverse understory that is characteristic of the ecosystem.

Education and Commitment. Education of the public regarding the current status of the longleaf pine ecosystem, its potential economic value, its outstanding biodiversity, and the role of fire in maintaining the system is an initial step in securing support for restoration (Landers et al. 1995). A primary need in this process is to promote the use of fire as an ecological force necessary for maintenance of this fire-dependent ecosystem. Frequent prescribed burning, including use of growing-season fires where appropriate, promotes the diversity and stability of these communities (Noss 1989). Many private landowners are concerned about the environment and will support restoration, if through the process they generate income from their land. Longleaf pine can be managed in an ecologically sensitive manner that generates income satisfactory to interest a landowner in restoration (Landers et al. 1990)

Determination of Success. One way to measure the success of the restoration process is to determine through periodic forest surveys if the area in the longleaf pine type increases. Another method is to determine if the production of longleaf pine nursery stock increases in relation to the other southern pines. Some would question whether an increase in area of longleaf pine plantations equates to an increase in ecosystem restoration. Certainly it takes more than planting trees to restore the ecosystem, but it is the critical first step. Recent research indicates that the productivity of an ecosystem is controlled to an overwhelming extent by the functional characteristics of the dominant plants (Grime 1997). So, with reestablishment and appropriate management, including the appropriate use of fire, restoration processes that include development of the typical diverse understory vegetation will begin.

CONCLUSIONS

Fire was an important component of the original longleaf pine ecosystem. Landscapes were characterized by open stands of mature pine with a savanna-like understory. This very biologically rich understory was typical for the ecosystem. Recent improvements in reforestation of longleaf pine has increased interest in restoring the ecosystem on many sites where it originally grew. It is recognized that fire must play an important role in the restoration process. Frequent use of fire hastens initiation of height growth, reduces undesirable competing vegetation, and stimulates growth and development of species that are a component of the understory. Fire is an important element in establishing the species and is a critical component of achieving and maintaining the biologically diverse understory that is characteristic of the ecosystem.

LITERATURE CITED

Barnett, J.P. 1992. The South's longleaf pine: It can rise again! Forests and People 41(4): 14-17.

Barnett, J.P. and J.M. McGilvray. 1997. Practical guidelines for producing longleaf pine seedlings in containers. USDA Forest Service General Tech. Report SRS-14. Southern Research Station, Asheville, NC. 28 p.

Boyer, W.D. 1990. *Pinus palustris* Mill. longleaf pine. *In* Silvics of North America. Vol. 1, Conifers, tech. coord. R.M. Burns and B.H. Honkala. USDA Forest Service, Washington, DC.

Croker, T.C. 1979. The longleaf pine story. Journal of Forest History 23: 32-43.

Frost, C.C. 1993. Four centuries of changing landscape patterns in the longleaf pine ecosystem. Proceedings, Tall Timbers Fire Ecology Conference 18. Tall Timbers, Tallahassee, FL.

Grelan, H.E. 1978. May burns stimulate growth of longleaf pine seedlings. USDA Forest Service Research Note SO-234. Southern Forest Experiment Station, New Orleans, LA. 5 p.

Grime, J.P. 1997. Biodiversity and ecosystem function: the debate deepens. Science 227(5330): 1260-1261.

Hardin, E.D. and D.L. White. 1989. Rare vascular plant taxa associated with wiregrass (*Aristida stricta*) in the southeastern United States. Natural Areas Journal 9: 234-245.

Kelly, J.F. and W.A. Bechtold. 1990. The longleaf pine resource. *In* Proceedings of the Symposium on the Management of longleaf pine, ed. R.M. Farrar, Jr. USDA Forest Service General Technical Report SO-75. Southern Forest Experiment Station, New Orleans, LA.

Landers, J.L. 1991. Disturbance influences on pine traits in the southeastern United States. Proceedings, Tall Timbers Fire Ecology Conference 17. Tall Timbers, Tallahassee, FL.

Landers, J.L., D.H. van Leer, and W.D. Boyer. 1995. The longleaf pine forests of the Southeast: Requiem or renaissance? Journal of Forestry 93: 39-44.

Landers, J.L., N.A. Byrd and R. Komarek. 1990. A holistic approach to managing longleaf pine communities. *In* Proceedings of the symposium on management of longleaf pine, ed. R.M. Farrar, Jr. USDA Forest Service General Technical Report SO-75. Southern Forest Experiment Station, New Orleans, LA.

McKee, W.H. 1982. Changes in soil fertility following prescribed burning on Coastal Plains pine sites. USDA Forest Service Research Paper SE-234. Southeastern Forest Experiment Station, Asheville, NC.

Noss, R.F. 1989. Longleaf pine and wiregrass: Keystone components of an endangered ecosystem. Natural Areas Journal 9: 234-235.

Oliver, C.D. 1992. Achieving and maintaining biodiversity and economic productivity. Journal of Forestry 90: 20-25.

Peet, R.K. and D.J. Allard. 1993. Longleaf pine-dominated vegetation of the southern Atlantic and eastern Gulf Coast region, USA. Proceedings, Tall Timbers Fire Ecology Conference 18. Tall Timbers, Tallahassee, FL.

Wahlenberg, W.G. 1946. Longleaf pine: Its use, ecology, regeneration, protection, growth, and management. C.L. Pack Foundation, Washington, DC.

Walker, J.L. 1993. Rare vascular plant taxa associated with the longleaf pine ecosystem. Proceedings, Tall Timbers Fire Ecology Conference 18. Tall Timbers, Tallahassee, FL.

Informational Analysis
of Forest Landscape Spatial Heterogeneity

Carlo Ricotta
Piermaria Corona
Marco Marchetti

SUMMARY. Under the perspective of forest ecosystem management, landscape is interpreted as a functioning structure. From an inventory and monitoring operational point of view, such an approach implies wise use of geographic information systems and remote sensing techniques enabling a global view of the territorial mosaic. From a methodological point of view, landscape ecology theory may be used as the assessment framework. Remotely sensed data provide excellent opportunities for the involved analyses, using both vegetation density measures and spatial statistics. The objective of this paper was to assess landscape spatial heterogeneity using an analysis method based on Shannon's information theoretic entropy applied to satellite remotely

Carlo Ricotta is affiliated with the Department of Plant Biology of Università di Roma "La Sapienza," piazzale Aldo Moro 5, 00185 Roma, Italy.

Piermaria Corona is Associate Professor of Forest Inventory at Istituto di Assestamento e Tecnologia Forestale of Università di Firenze, via San Bonaventura 13, 50145 Firenze, Italy.

Marco Marchetti is Adjunct Professor of Forest Inventory, Corso di laurea in Scienze Forestali, Università di Palermo, Via Roma, 23, 92010 Bivona (Agrigento), Italy.

The work was coordinated by C. Ricotta and partially funded by the Italian National Council of Research (CNR) under the Project "Procedure innovative per la classificazione di tipologie forestali tramite analisi delle relazioni spaziali rilevate con immagini da satellite" (Project leader: P. Corona).

[Haworth co-indexing entry note]: "Informational Analysis of Forest Landscape Spatial Heterogeneity." Ricotta, Carlo, Piermaria Corona, and Marco Marchetti. Co-published simultaneously in *Journal of Sustainable Forestry* (Food Products Press, an imprint of The Haworth Press, Inc.) Vol. 9, No. 1/2, 1999, pp. 97-106; and: *Contested Issues of Ecosystem Management* (ed: Piermaria Corona, and Boris Zeide) Food Products Press, an imprint of The Haworth Press, Inc., 1999, pp. 97-106. Single or multiple copies of this article are available for a fee from The Haworth Document Delivery Service [1-800-342-9678, 9:00 a.m. - 5:00 p.m. (EST). E-mail address: getinfo@haworthpressinc.com].

97

sensed inputs of plant biomass. A forested mountainous landscape of
Central Italy was examined as a case study. In this area, anthropogenic
disturbance resulted as opposing the natural tendency of vegetation towards an horizontally homogeneous landscape giving way to a micro-
heterogeneous structure composed of long-term stratification of small
patches. The proposed analysis method proves to be simply refinable by
more finely classifying land cover types to enable a more thoroughly
landscape texture properties linkage to ecological processes. *[Article
copies available for a fee from The Haworth Document Delivery Service:
1-800-342-9678. E-mail address: getinfo@haworthpressinc.com <Website:
http://www.haworthpressinc.com>]*

KEYWORDS. Landscape spatial heterogeneity, plant biomass, satellite remote sensing, information theoretic entropy, Central Italy

INTRODUCTION

The increased concern for forest ecosystem management has created
extended information needs. In such a context, the role of forest inventory and monitoring is enhanced, and objectives refined (Corona and
Marchetti 1998). Under the perspective of forest ecosystem management, landscape is interpreted as a functioning structure. A holistic
and synthetic knowledge approach is then required. From an inventory
and monitoring operational point of view, such an approach implies
wise use of geographic information systems (GIS) and remote sensing
(RS) techniques so enabling a global view of the landscape, including
forest borders, clearings, open woodland, etc. From a methodological
point of view, landscape ecology theory may be used as the assessment framework.

Landscape structure is largely determined by the type, number and
size of the patches. However, the spatial configuration among the
patches may be just as important (Forman and Godron 1986). Because
landscape heterogeneity is a spatial phenomenon, quantitative measures of spatial structure are needed to improve understanding of
landscape pattern and dynamics. A natural way to describe and
compare landscape structure is by measuring the shape of patches
within a landscape, or other spatial attributes, using RS and GIS techniques. In such a perspective, for the most used satellite RS images,
like those from Landsat Thematic Mapper (TM), texture analysis of
forested environments can provide useful information for a wide vari-

ety of applications, due to the relatively high local variance at the adopted spatial resolutions (Woodcock and Strahler 1987).

The main objective of this paper is to assess landscape spatial heterogeneity using satellite remotely sensed inputs of plant biomass. A wide variety of texture algorithms can be performed to assess landscape complexity from RS images (Riitters et al. 1995). In this work, the use of Shannon's information theoretic entropy (Shannon and Weaver 1963) is proposed. A forested mountainous landscape of Central Italy is examined as a case study.

CASE STUDY AREA

The selected study area is located across the municipalities of Trevi nel Lazio and Filettino (Central Italy). The area is roughly 130 km^2 wide, and due to its environmental importance was designated in 1983 as part of the Natural Park of the Simbruini Mountains. The relief is approximately 1,600 m a.s.l.; the highest point is 2,156 m a.s.l. The slopes are particularly steep along the drainage lines, but more gentle in the alluvial plain of the Aniene River and in the numerous karst plateaus of the area.

The anthropic landscape is complex and stratified, as in every area of long-standing settlement. The most evident stratification can be seen near the villages of Trevi and Filettino where the superimposition of new structures on the historical pattern gives way to a new landscape, often disordered and degraded. The karst-plateaus were traditionally used as grazing grounds after the opening of large clearings; some have been recently converted to winter recreation areas. After the Second World War, agriculture has diminished in importance as a full-time activity but continues on a part-time basis in order to supplement income from other activities. This gives way in a widespread fragmentation of properties which has resulted in abandonment of the more inaccessible fields. Nevertheless, despite the intense human activity, 66 percent of the study area is still covered by forests (Regione Lazio 1988).

The forests in the lower-mountain domain are dominated by *Melittio-Ostrietum carpinifoliae* Avena-Blasi-1980 phytosociological association. In general, *Melittio-Ostrietum typicum* covers a broad strip of the lower-mountain domain ranging from 700 to 1100 m. Therefore, at the lower elevations, thermophilous species, such as *Acer monspessu-*

lanum L., are present, while at the higher elevations the species of the *Fagetalia sylvaticae* Pawl.-1928 phytosociological association become more common. On the north-facing slopes, besides *Ostrya carpinifolia* Scop., *Carpinus betulus* L. and *Tilia platiphyllos* Scop., *Populus tremula* L. and *Quercus cerris* L. are also present, while the understory is characterized by several elements of the *Fagetalia sylvaticae*. The south-facing slopes of the lower-mountain domain are characterized by the *Cytiso sessilifolii-Quercetum pubescentis* Blasi-Feoli-Avena-1982 phytosociological association. In the past, these forests have been largely degraded and replaced by crops and pasture lands now abandoned. In the upper-mountain domain beech woods belonging to the *Polysticho-Fagetum* Feoli-Lagonegro-1982 phytosociological association are dominant: they are dense forests dominated by *Fagus sylvatica* L. sporadically associated with other tree species, such as *Acer pseudoplatanus* L., *Acer platanoides* L. and *Sorbus aria*. The transition zone between the *Melittio-Ostryetum carpinifoliae* and the *Polysticho-Fagetum* associations is represented by a narrow strip of *Aquifolio-Fagetum* Gentile-1969 association which includes different species of *Quercetalia pubescenti-petraeae* Br.-Bl.(1931)-em.-Tx.-1937, besides *Fagus sylvatica*. Small portions of the study area are represented by *Pinus nigra* Arnold, *Abies alba* Miller and *Cupressus sempervirens* L. plantations.

MATERIALS AND METHODS

Basic material for this study was a georeferenced NDVI Landsat 5 TM scene (nominal pixel resolution of 30 m). Remotely sensed vegetation indices are generally a very effective tool for environmental resource monitoring and to quantify different ecological events. NDVI, the normalized difference of the bi-directional reflectances in the red and near-infrared bands, has become the primary tool for accurate description of vegetation cover due to his strong relationship to the amount of absorbed photosynthetically active radiation, total biomass and fractional vegetation cover (Chong et al. 1993): increasing positive values of this index indicate increasing green vegetation and negative values indicate unvegetated areas.

Digital counts of the Landsat bands TM3 and TM4 were radiometrically calibrated into spectral radiances usirig the gain and offset values proposed by Markham and Barker (1986). The NDVI was then generated from the calibrated TM data as NDVI = $(L_{NIR} - L_{RED})/(L_{NIR} + L_{RED})$, where L_{NIR} and L_{RED} are respectively the spectral radiances in the near-infrared and red bands (Figure 1). The computed NDVI ranges from -1.0 to 1.0 but were rescaled to 0-200 with a value 100 equal to a computed NDVI of 0. To overcome the high spectral variability of the resulting scene, the NDVI image was subjected to a smoothing filter with a neighborhood function of $5'5$ pixels.

Color near-infrared photographs were used to stratify the NDVI image into non-overlapping land cover classes. The cover types used in this study were simply forest vs. non-forest, representing respectively the natural landscape as opposed to the disturbance patches

FIGURE 1. The NDVI Landsat 5 TM scene from 29 July 1993 used to assess forest landscape spatial heterogeneity in the case study area. Darker pixels represent forest vegetation cover.

related to human activity (e.g., urban, pasture, cropland, abandoned cropland, brush).

A stratified random sampling of 5-by-5-pixel samples was performed on the stratified NDVI image. The resulting sample consisted of 479 forest samples and 789 non-forest samples. For each sample, a texture index based on the Shannon's information theoretic entropy was calculated to capture the spatial content of plant biomass heterogeneity at local scale.

SHANNON'S ENTROPY AS A LANDSCAPE INDICATOR

Let us consider the distribution of a numerical variable in a finite set N over a sub-landscape (sample) X that is systematically tessellated into equal sized pixels. We assume the pixels are independent and each pixel is associated to a measured value nk in N: N = {nk, k Î[1, ½N½]}, where ½N½ is the number of elements of N (Le Hégarat-Mascle et al. 1997). For instance, as in our case, N may be the set of integer NDVI values ranging from 0 to 200. Using natural logarithms the Shannon entropy H(X) of the sub-landscape can be calculated as:

$$H(X) = -\sum_{n_k \in N} P(n_k) \ln[P(n_k)] \qquad (1)$$

where P(nk) is the probability of the pixels of the sub-landscape associated to the measured value nk such that $0 \leq P(nk) \leq 1$ and

$$\sum_{n_k \in N} P(n_k) = 1 \qquad (2)$$

Notice that maximum entropy is obtained in case of equiprobability. In other words, if P(nk) = 1/|N| for every k, H(X)max = ln[1/|N|]. In contrast, minimum entropy is obtained if there is a value having its probability equal to 1 (the probabilities of all the other values being null), which implies H(X)min = 0.

From an interpretation point of view, Shannon's entropy in an information theoretical sense relates to its thermodynamical meaning. It assumes stability accumulation as index of the approachment to natural equilibrium conditions, prescinding from other considerations (Corona and Pignatti 1996). Natural conditions should be referenced to the order that a given natural system would have if any intervention by modern man had not been operated. In the examined framework, the information content of a given system may be therefore considered as a measure of system's human-induced disorder. The case in which all sets have almost the same frequency evidences a highly disordered system, while the case in which all elements are concentrated in one set reflects a highly organized system.

RESULTS AND DISCUSSION

Shannon entropy distributions of both examined land cover types (forest; non-forest) are shown in Figure 2. The stratification of entropy values using the cover types as grouping variable with the Mann-Whitney non-parametric procedure (SAS 1991) proves that texture provides significant distinction between forest and non-forest at the 0.001 significance level.

As hypothesized, forest cover, which is characterized by a relatively high homogeneity in biomass spatial distribution, presents an homogeneous texture characterized by lower entropy values. Furthermore, due to the general high performance of almost any texture algorithm in edge/ecotones detection (Johnston and Bonde 1989; Rubin 1990), the higher values in the entropy distribution of forest cover result from those samples falling in the proximity of forest edges or at lower altitudes where human pressure is more pronounced. Due to the high levels of patch micro-heterogeneity introduced by anthropogenic disturbance, the entropy of the non-forest cover type, which consists of all the land uses more impacted by human activities, generally shows higher values.

Landscape fragmentation is probably one of the most important human-induced impacts on forest ecosystems (Marchetti 1996). When undisturbed, forest vegetation tends to develop in an anti-enthropic direction by saturating the natural environment until it reaches a maximum of biomass or potential energy compatible with available resources (Forman and Godron 1986). Consequently, when unconstrained by human activity, forested environments tend to progress towards spatial horizontal homogeneity forming a coarse grained landscape with patches resulting from spatial variations in physical factors.

The informational analysis carried out to characterize landscape

FIGURE 2. Histogram of the entropy values distribution from (A) the forest cover type and (B) the non-forest cover.

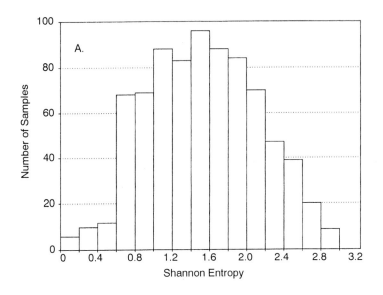

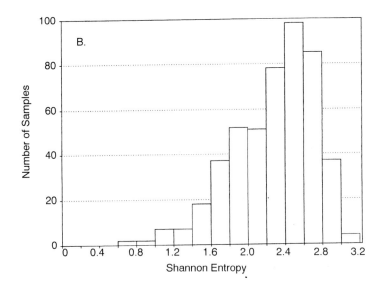

texture outlines the essence of the relationships between plant biomass spatial variability and anthropogenic disturbance on the examined landscape of Central Italy at the scale of Landsat TM data. The final result is an environment in which there is a natural tendency of the vegetation towards a high level of homogeneity in biomass distribution opposed by a secular man-caused tendency towards a high contrast micro-heterogeneity. Generally speaking, anthropogenic disturbance tends to oppose the natural tendency of vegetation towards an horizontally homogeneous landscape giving way to a micro-heterogeneous structure composed of long-term stratification of small patches.

CONCLUSIONS

RS data provide excellent opportunities for forest ecosystem assessment using both vegetation density measures and spatial statistics. In such a context, the contribution of the present study was to survey human-induced heterogeneity within a forested mountainous landscape through an informational analysis on remotely sensed data.

The proposed analysis method may be performed at different scale levels. It is also easily refinable by breaking the land cover types into finer classes to link more thourougly landscape texture properties to ecological processes.

LITERATURE CITED

Chong, D.L., Mougin, E. and J.P. Gastellu-Etchegorry. 1993. Relating the global vegetation index to net primary productivity and actual evapotranspiration over Africa. International Journal of Remote Sensing 14:1517-1546.

Corona, P. and G. Pignatti. 1996. Assessing and comparing forest plantations proximity to natural conditions. Journal of Sustainable Forestry 4:37-46.

Corona, P. and M. Marchetti. 1998. Towards an Effective Integration of Forest Inventories and Natural Resources Surveys: the Italian Perspective. Proceedings, Integrated tools for Natural Resources Inventories in the 21th Century, Boise, ID (in press).

Forman, R.T.T. and M. Godron, 1986. Landscape Ecology. Wily, New York.

Johnston, C.A. and J. Bonde. 1989. Quantitative analysis of ecotones using a geographic information system. Photogrammetric Engineering and Remote Sensing 11:1643-1647.

Le Hégarat-Mascle, S., Vidal-Madjar, D., Taconet, O. and M. Zribi. 1997. Application of Shannon information theory to a comparison between L- and C-band

SIR-C polarimetric data versus incidence angle. Remote Sensing of Environment 60:121-130.

Marchetti, M. 1996. Analisi spaziale di dati telerilevati per la valutazione della diversità nei paesaggi forestali. Atti, 1$ Congresso IAED, Perugia. Italy. Quaderno IAED 6:71-78.

Markham, B.L. and J.L. Barker. 1986. Landsat MSS and TM post-calibration dynamic ranges. Exoatmospheric reflectances and at-satellite temperatures. Landsat Technical Notes 1:3-8.

Regione Lazio. 1988. Indagine Conoscitiva sui Boschi del Parco Naturale Regionale dei Monti Simbruini. Ufficio Parchi e Riserve Naturali, Roma.

Riitters, K.H., O'Neill, R.V., Hunsaker, C.T., Wickham, J.D., Yankee, D.H., Timmins, S.P., Jones, K.B. and D.L. Jackson. 1995. A factor analysis of landscape pattern and structure metrics. Landscape Ecology 10:23-39.

Rubin, T. 1990. Analysis of radar texture vith variograms and other simplified descriptors. Proceedings of the ASPRS Symposium, Image Processing '89, Sparks, Nevada, American Society of Photogrammetry and Remote Sensing, Falls Church, Virginia.

SAS. 1991. Statistical Analysis System, Version 6.03. SAS Institute Inc., Cary, North Carolina.

Shannon, C.E. and W. Weaver. 1963. The Mathematical Theory of Communication. University of Illinois Press, Urbana, Illinois.

Woodcock, C.E. and A.H. Strahler. 1987. The factor of scale in remote sensing. Remote Sensing of Environment 21:311-332.

Place of Intensive Forestry
in Ecosystem Management

David R. Bower

SUMMARY. As population increases, the needs for products from the forest increase, along with the needs for recreation, wildlife, and esthetics. Although some of these products can also be produced by substitutes, such as plastic, steel, or aluminum, forest products have the desirable property of coming from a renewable resource, that is economically produced, and has positive environmental aspects. While use of forests for products does not preclude their use for recreation, and other nonproduct values, setting aside large tracts solely for recreation obviously can constrain total forest product yields. It is proposed that emphasis should be placed on intensive plantation management, or production forests, to significantly improve product flows to meet people's needs, while freeing other areas for alternative uses. Examples are given to show how genetically improved stock, seedling culture, site preparation, management of competing grass and hardwoods, fertilization, and thinning, can be used to increase product yields from intensively managed forests. The proposed forest management practices are also conducive to good wild life production, recreation, soil stability, and water quality. *[Article copies available for a fee from The Haworth Document Delivery Service: 1-800-342-9678. E-mail address: getinfo@ haworthpressinc.com <Website: http://www.haworthpressinc.com>]*

David R. Bower is Leader of Silviculture and Wood Quality Project, Southern Forestry Research Department, Weyerhaeuser Company, P.O. Box 1060, Hot Springs, AR 71902.

The author wishes to thank the Southern Forest Experiment Station, USFS, and the Rice Land Lumber Company, for their participation in the Merryville Study, and the Southwest Research and Extension Center, Hope, Arkansas, for assistance in the "Incremental Growth Gains" study.

[Haworth co-indexing entry note]: "Place of Intensive Forestry in Ecosystem Management." Bower, David R. Co-published simultaneously in *Journal of Sustainable Forestry* (Food Products Press, an imprint of The Haworth Press, Inc.) Vol. 9, No. 1/2, 1999, pp. 107-115; and: *Contested Issues of Ecosystem Management* (ed: Piermaria Corona, and Boris Zeide) Food Products Press, an imprint of The Haworth Press, Inc., 1999, pp. 107-115. Single or multiple copies of this article are available for a fee from The Haworth Document Delivery Service [1-800-342-9678, 9:00 a.m. - 5:00 p.m. (EST). E-mail address: getinfo@haworthpressinc.com].

KEYWORDS. Ecosystem management, intensive forestry, pine plantations

COMMODITY-PRODUCTION FORESTRY

Staebler (1993) suggested that focusing on "commodity-production forestry" as a dominant use would allow foresters to grow timber crops "in such quantities that the pressures to produce wood in forests set aside for other dominant uses would be greatly reduced." Sedjo and Botkin (1997) suggested that if planted forests could produce 10 m^3/ hectare annually, that only 0.15 billion hectares of plantation, or roughly 4% of the global forest, would be required to produce the world's industrial wood production of 1.5 billion cubic meters. Drawing on a large experimental data base for planted loblolly pine (*Pinus taeda* L.), in the Southern U.S., this report shows that medium site intensively managed plantations should produce up to 9.5 m^3/hectare/year.

INTENSIVE PLANTATION MANAGEMENT

Site Quality and Early Treatments–Site quality varies widely across the Southern U.S., dependent on soils and climate. Published yield tables show volume productivity increasing directly with site quality or site index. Financial incentives for intensive management typically increase with increased site quality. Early growth rate and even long-term site quality can be enhanced by contour ripping (producing improved planting spots for seedlings in rocky soils), bedding on wetter sites, grass control (reduced competition for seedling) and fertilization in beds. Seedling quality can also enhance seedling survival and early growth.

Plantation Spacing and Thinning Level–Bower and Baldwin (1992) reported on a 38-year old loblolly plantation in Southwest, Louisiana, USA, grown at a wide range of initial planting spacings (1.8 × 1.8 m^2 to 3.7 × 3.7 m^2) and subsequently thinned (age 18, 23, 28, 32, 38) to a wide range of residual basal area (BA) levels (13.8 m^2/ha to 27.6 m^2/ha). Narrow spacing provided more total yield thru age 38 on the thinned plots but less total yield on non-thinned plots (Table 1). As expected, tree diameter is enhanced by wider initial spacings and heavier thinnings on this 19.5 m (age 25) site index land.

Another example of tradeoffs in tree diameter vs. volume per hectare by residual thinning level is provided by the Red Cut Thinning Study in Southwest Arkansas, USA, Figures 1 and 2, (Bower 1995).

TABLE 1. Final Diameter at Breast Height (DBH), Largest 125 Trees/ha, and Total Yield, Age 38, by Initial Spacing and Residual BA, for the Loblolly Pine Plantation at Merryville, Louisiana, USA

	DBH and Total Yield[1] by Residual BA and Initial Spacing					
Residual BA Level	DBH (9 cm) – Top 125 T/ha			Total Yield (m³/ha)		
(m²/ha)	1.8 × 1.8	2.7 × 2.7	3.7 × 3.7	1.8 × 1.8	2.7 × 2.7	3.7 × 3.7
13.8	34.0	37.0	39.2	350	330	272
18.4	31.5	34.3	37.2	353	305	309
23.0	31.9	34.6	38.1	395	364	362
27.6	32.6	34.6	---	421	402	---
Controls	30.0	34.1	35.7	267	326	331

[1]Yield of all thinnings plus final standing volume.

FIGURE 1

RED CUT THINNING LEVEL STUDY
DBH (CROP TREES–125 TR/HA) BY AGE AND STOCKING

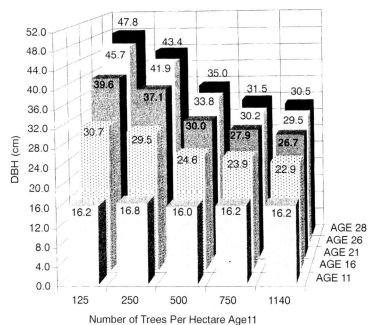

FIGURE 2

RED CUT THINNING LEVEL STUDY
Summary of Sawlog, Chip-N-Saw, and Top Volume
(Cubic Meter/Hectare) by Thinning Level–Age 28

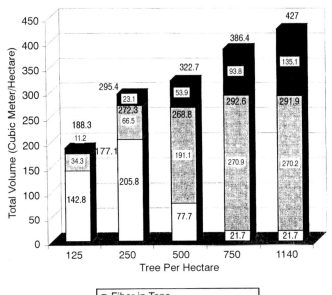

At age 11, when Red Cut was thinned, the residual diameter, of 125 crop trees per hectare averaged ≈16.2 cm for all thinning levels. Figure 1 shows the responsiveness of loblolly pine to stocking level, such that by age 28, tree diameter ranged from 47.8 cm for 125 trees per hectare to 30.5 cm for 1140 trees per hectare. Figure 2 shows that the higher residual stocking levels provided much higher standing volume at age 28, ranging from 427 m^3/hectare at 1140 trees/hectare to 188 m^3/hectare at 125 trees/hectare. Potential solidwood product volume (5.0 meter logs with small end diameter > 15.2 cm) varied much less from the 250 tree/hectare treatment to the 1140 tree/hectare treatment on this 20.7 meter site index land. The highest residual stocking level at Red Cut provided 15.8 m^3/hectare per year annual yield, with fertilization and weed control but with use of regular unimproved seed source.

Impacts of Hardwood Control and Genetics–A cooperative study in Southwest Arkansas, USA, between Weyerhaeuser Company and the University of Arkansas Southwest Research and Extension Center, Hope, Arkansas, compares incremental growth gains for planted loblolly pine (3 × 3 m² spacing) from genetics and hardwood control (9 year results) are reported (Bower and Colvin 1994). Hardwoods were controlled at age 3 using 187 grams Arsenal per 45 liters of water. Figure 3 shows an average diameter gain of 2.5 cm (16%) at age 13 from planting North Carolina improved family NC1 vs. Arkansas regular seedlings, and an additional 2.3 cm for control of hardwood competition. Similarly, average height gains for genetics are 2.1 meters, with an additional 0.5 meter gain for hardwood control (Figure 4). The diameter and height gains led to volume gains for genetics of 43 m³/hectare, with an additional volume gain of 49 m³/hectare for hardwood control (Figure 5).

Predicting Gains from Intensive Management–Incremental gains

FIGURE 3

HOPE COOP STUDY AGE 13
SEED SOURCE AND HARDWOOD CONTROL

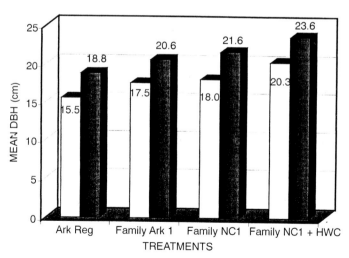

FIGURE 4

HOPE COOP STUDY AGE 13
SEED SOURCE AND HARDWOOD CONTROL

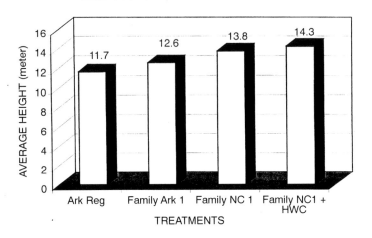

FIGURE 5

HOPE COOP STUDY AGE 13
SEED SOURCE AND HARDWOOD CONTROL TOTAL STEM VOLUME

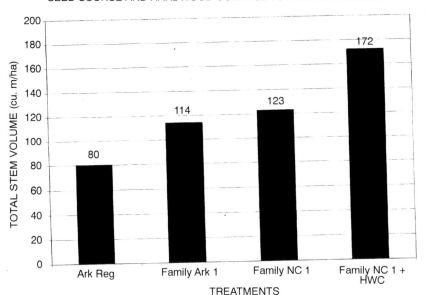

TABLE 2. Assumptions for Gains from Intensive Management

Thinning	• Thin at Age 17 to 420 Trees/ha; d/D = .95
	• Thin at Age 27 to 10.4 m²/ha BA; d/D = .95
	• Use Model to Quantify Tradeoff in DBH vs. vol/ha
Hardwood Control	• Reduce % HDW BA from 20% to 5%
	• Assume similar competition from a unit of hardwood BA as a unit of pine BA
	• Site index improves by 0.5 meters
Fertilization	• Fertilize at ages 17, 22, 27, 32
	• Gain expectation is ≈ 14 m³/ha/treatment
Genetics	• Site index improves by 2.2 meters

from thinning, hardwood control, fertilization, and genetics were projected to age 42 via a proprietary growth and yield model. This projection assumed an initial stocking of 990 trees per hectare at age 7, and a base site index of 19.8 meters. Table 2 provides a summary of the assumptions for thinning, hardwood control, fertilization, and genetics, which were based on the Hope study, described in this report, as well as on other studies. Figure 6 shows substantial gains in diameter ranging from 27.9 cm for the unthinned base case to 42.2 cm for the most intensive treatment, a 51% gain! Similarly volumes in Figure 7 range from 266 m³/hectare (6.3 m³/ha/year) to 397 m³/hectare (9.5 m³/ha/year) a 49% gain! Results show a tremendous opportunity for plantations to meet forest products needs, while freeing other areas for alternative uses!

CONCLUSIONS

Growth and yield simulations showed that with intensive management, including thinning, hardwood control, fertization and genetics; medium site loblolly pine plantations can produced 9.5 m³/ha/year. With wide spread adoption of intensive management practices, only a small fraction of global forests would be needed to meet the world's annual industrial wood production needs and pressure to produce wood in forests set aside for other dominant uses would be reduced.

FIGURE 6

GAINS FROM INTENSIVE MANAGEMENT–AGE 42
BASE AGE 25 SI = 19.8 M; AGE 7 STOCKING = 990 TR/HA

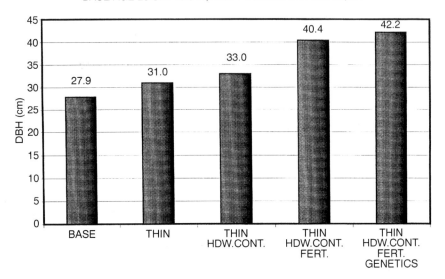

FIGURE 7

GAINS FROM INTENSIVE MANAGEMENT–AGE 42
BASE AGE 25 SI = 19.8 M; AGE 7 STOCKING = 990 TR/HA

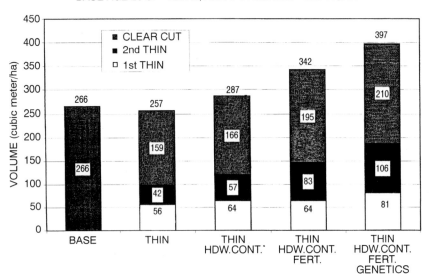

LITERATURE CITED

Bower, D.R. 1995. Effects of Thinning Timing and Level on Loblolly Pine Volume and Diameter Growth Response–The Biological Basis for Thinning. Western Mensurationist's Meeting, Delta Whistler Resort, Whistler, B.C., Canada. Unpublished Report.

Bower, D.R., and V.C. Baldwin. 1992. Effects of Initial Planting Spacing and Subsequent Thinning Levels on Stand Dynamics, Growth, and Long Term Production, for Loblolly Pine, in Southwest, Louisiana, USA. Proceedings Centennial IUFRO Conference, Berlin, Germany.

Bower, D.R., and Bob Colvin. 1994. Effects of Management Intensity on Loblolly Pine Plantation Growth. IUFRO Conference on Mixed Stands Research Plots, Measurements, and Results, Lousa/Coimbra, Portugal.

Sedjo, Roger A., and Daniel Botkin. 1997. Using Forest Plantations to Spare Natural Forests, Environment, 39:14-20, 30.

Staebler, G.R. 1993. Have We Milked the Sacred Cow Dry? Journal of Forestry 91(10): 60.

Ecosystem Management in Tropical Timber Plantations: Satisfying Economic, Conservation, and Social Objectives

R. J. Keenan
D. Lamb
J. Parrotta
J. Kikkawa

SUMMARY. Management of tropical timber plantations is generally based on a single-product output, high-input model, often using an exotic species, that has been successfully used for plantation timber production in many temperate regions. This intensive model may be appropriate in areas designated solely for wood production but where the aim is to produce a wider range of conservation benefits and maintain more ecosystem functions, alternative plantation management ap-

R. J. Keenan is affiliated with Queensland Forestry Research Institute, P.O. Box 1138, Atherton, Q. 4883 Australia, and CRC Tropical Rainforest Ecology and Management, Cairns, Q. Australia.

D. Lamb is affiliated with CRC Tropical Rainforest Ecology and Management, Cairns, Q. Australia, and Botany Department, University of Queensland, St. Lucia, Q. 4072, Australia.

J. Parrotta is affiliated with the International Institute of Tropical Forestry, USDA Forest Service, Rio Piedras, Puerto Rico, 00928-5000.

J. Kikkawa is affiliated with CRC Tropical Rainforest Ecology and Management, Cairns, Q. Australia, and Zoology Department, University of Queensland, St. Lucia, Q. 4072, Australia.

[Haworth co-indexing entry note]: "Ecosystem Management in Tropical Timber Plantations: Satisfying Economic, Conservation, and Social Objectives." Keenan, R. J. et al. Co-published simultaneously in *Journal of Sustainable Forestry* (Food Products Press, an imprint of The Haworth Press, Inc.) Vol. 9, No. 1/2, 1999, pp. 117-134; and: *Contested Issues of Ecosystem Management* (ed: Piermaria Corona, and Boris Zeide) Food Products Press, an imprint of The Haworth Press, Inc., 1999, pp. 117-134. Single or multiple copies of this article are available for a fee from The Haworth Document Delivery Service [1-800-342-9678, 9:00 a.m. - 5:00 p.m. (EST). E-mail address: getinfo@haworthpressinc.com].

proaches will be required. In this paper we describe some alternative management options for tropical forest plantations, incorporating ecosystem management concepts, that can potentially result in a wider range ecosystem benefits from tropical landscapes. Some of these practices have been used by plantation management agencies for some time. Others have been applied on a small scale or are still to be tested operationally. Options include: (1) consideration of the forest landscape and management of the matrix in which the plantation is established, (2) the use of native rather than exotic species, (3) using mixed species plantations rather than monocultures, (4) using the plantation to facilitate natural understorey regeneration, and (5) incorporating more structural and compositional diversity in plantations for wildlife habitat. *[Article copies available for a fee from The Haworth Document Delivery Service: 1-800-342-9678. E-mail address: getinfo@haworthpressinc.com <Website: http://www.haworthpressinc.com>]*

KEYWORDS. Biodiversity, mixed species plantations, forest restoration, wildlife habitat

INTRODUCTION

Reducing the rate of decline in biological diversity while maintaining reasonable living standards for an expanding human population is a major conservation dilemma. Many industrialised countries have achieved their present levels of social and economic development through the capitalisation of natural resources and reducing their native forest estate, and this model has often been proposed to meet development needs of rapidly growing populations in the tropics (Kahn and McDonald 1997). However, development of tropical landscapes is problematic because of the comparatively greater loss of biological diversity likely to result from deforestation in the tropics compared with temperate regions and because many tropical landscapes have a high susceptibility to decline in productive capacity when developed for intensive agriculture (Kahn and McDonald 1997).

Timber plantations are seen as a major potential contributor to economic development in many parts of the tropics. In 1990 there was an estimated 15.6 million ha of industrial forest plantations in the tropics, and 28.2 million ha of non-industrial plantations, including fuelwood plantations. The rate of plantation establishment is increasing, largely for wood production purposes. Policies for the development of forest plantations in tropical developing countries usually target previously-cleared or degraded forest lands but there is also considerable conversion of natural forest to plantations.

Development and implementation of policies for the sustainable development of tropical landscapes will require a complex mix of economic, political and ecological solutions. For forested landscapes there are three broad land use options that can be applied in varying proportions to meet different policy objectives (Seymour and Hunter 1992): nature reserves, extensively-managed and intensively-managed forests. A viable and representative system of reserves is the core of any conservation strategy but there is increasing recognition that conservation objectives cannot be achieved through reserves alone. Management of vegetation outside reserves will be crucial to the survival of many forest dwelling species (Hale and Lamb 1997, Lindenmeyer and Recher 1998). Extensive management involves managing for a wider range of conservation and environmental benefits in addition to the production of timber or other resources and is generally adopted in natural forests. Intensive management usually involves plantations managed to maximise the production of timber, but plantations (or intensively-managed natural regrowth) can also contribute significant environmental benefits such as watershed protection and soil conservation.

The concept of 'forest ecosystem management' has been the subject of considerable debate among scientists and forest managers (Swanson and Franklin 1992, Gerlach and Bengston 1994, Irland 1994, Wiant 1995, and Gilmore 1997). It is generally considered to involve managing forests according to sound ecological principles in order to provide a continuing supply of wide range of ecosystem goods, services and benefits. It embodies many components of the traditional forest management concept of 'multiple-use' but also encompasses a more holistic, community-oriented, ecologically and scientifically-based, resource-stewardship philosophy (Kimmins 1997).

The combination of highly-weathered soils, high rainfall, and high temperatures often found in the tropics imposes particular limitations on land management. Traditional land use practices have generally evolved to accommodate these constraints. For example, shifting cultivation and land rotation with bush fallowing is often regarded as an exploitative and destructive practice, but is, in fact a highly-evolved and specialised technique developed by forest dwelling communities in response to the limitations imposed on broad-scale agriculture by the tropical forest environment (Weischet and Caviedes 1993). Similarly, forest scientists and managers working in the tropics for a century or more have developed a considerable body of ecological knowledge that can be used as a basis for ecosystem management in the tropics (Bruenig 1996). However the application of sustainable management systems has been relatively rare for a range of political, economic and social reasons (Poore et al. 1989).

Management of tropical timber plantations is generally based on the single-product output, high-inputs model often using an exotic species, that has been successfully used for plantation timber production in many temperate regions. This intensive model may be appropriate in areas designated solely for wood production although, given the environmental limitations outlined above, it may not be successful in many parts of the tropics (Jordan 1993). Where the aim is to maintain a wider range of ecosystem benefits, alternative plantation management approaches will be required (Bass 1997).

In this paper we describe some alternative management options for tropical forest plantations, incorporating ecosystem management concepts, that can potentially result in a wider range ecosystem benefits from tropical landscapes. Some of these practices have been used by plantation management agencies for some time. Others have been applied on a small scale or are still to be tested operationally. Options include: (1) consideration of the forest landscape and management of the matrix in which the plantation is established, (2) the use of native rather than exotic species, (3) using mixed species plantations rather than monocultures, (4) using the plantation to facilitate natural understorey regeneration, and (5) incorporating more structural and compositional diversity in plantations for wildlife habitat.

LANDSCAPE-LEVEL MANAGEMENT

Plantation development in the tropics is taking place on lands where intact forest is being cleared, or where the previous vegetation has been cleared in the past for another land use. By retaining existing native vegetation, or by restoring natural vegetation on previously-cleared sites, the plantation can be embedded within a matrix of natural vegetation. This results in maintenance of a variety of environmental and conservation functions.

Protection of riparian zones is now a common feature of forest plantation practice. These areas are targeted for retention or restoration of natural vegetation within a production plantation because riparian buffers help maintain water quality and reduce soil erosion, and because they are generally the most productive sites within a landscape and provide habitat for a greater diversity of wildlife. Strips of vegetation can also be retained or established to connect blocks of remnant vegetation within the plantation between areas that are too steep or rocky for plantation development. These bands break large plantation areas into smaller blocks or compartments and the greater floristic and structural diversity of the matrix allows a wider variety of species to persist in the landscape (Gepp 1986, Suckling et al. 1976) and provides for connectivity between different landscape units (Forman 1995) which can signficantly increase the conservation value of a plantation. The maintenance of this matrix of more natural vegetation may result in some loss of plantation production. However, this is generally outweighed by benefits such as clean water and assistance with fire control.

USING NATIVE SPECIES

Tropical plantation projects have largely used a relatively narrow set of exotic species from the genera *Pinus*, *Eucalyptus*, *Acacia* or *Tectona*. Many tropical species in these genera have a range of advantages that make them suited to domestication as plantation species. These include:

- tolerance of a wide range of water and nutrient-limited situations,
- ease of establishment and rapid early growth,
- small, 'orthodox' seeds that can be easily transported and stored,
- ease of propagation by a range of means, and
- utility for a range of products.

Exotic species have been particularly valuable in forest establishment on badly degraded sites where it has often been difficult or impossible to establish native species.

Using native tree species instead of exotic species in plantation monocultures increases the conservation value of a plantation because a local species is more likely to be used as habitat by local wildlife. Using native species can also result in greater natural regeneration in the plantation understorey (see below). Many native species may also have a higher market or social value to the local community and using such species can make a plantation project more socially acceptable.

Testing of tree species for their potential in plantations has been occurring for many years (Streets 1962). For example, teak (*Tectona grandis*) has been successfully grown in plantations within and beyond its range since 1941 (Brown, Nambiar, and Cossalter 1997). High value species from the family Meliaceae (in genera such as *Swietenia, Khaya, Cedrela* and *Toona*) have also been planted across substantial areas, but have generally only been successful outside the range of native insect pests. However, high-value rainforest timbers have usually been readily and cheaply available from native forests and there has been little incentive to invest capital resources in establishing plantations of these species. These sources are now declining rapidly and there is increased interest in their development in plantations. There is also a growing interest in using a wider range of ecologically-beneficial and socially-acceptable species, and species testing has increased in recent years (Appanah and Weinland 1993, Butterfield and Fisher 1994, Butterfield 1995).

However, the capacity to use many rainforest species in plantation programs has been limited by difficulties with collection, storage and germination of fleshy-fruited seeds and other nursery propagation, pest and disease or silvicultural problems. With appropriate research (e.g., Knowles and Parrotta 1995) these problems are not insurmountable and there is an urgent need to expand our knowledge of plantation production ecology and appropriate silvicultural techniques to a wider range of tropical species.

MIXED SPECIES PLANTATIONS

Planting a mixture of species in a plantation has obvious benefits for increasing plantation diversity. Mixtures have been suggested as a management technique for tropical plantations for some time, but there are few successful operational examples (Wormald 1992). Mixtures can range from simple arrangements, such as alternate rows of two or more species, through to random mixtures of many species. Besides increasing within-stand diversity the potential benefits of mixtures over monocultures include:

Greater production–Species mixtures can potentially produce a greater amount of biomass per unit area by reducing competition between individuals and more fully utilising the site (Montagnini et al. 1995, Kelty and Cameron 1995). Mixing species with differing light requirements can result in canopy partitioning and a greater capture of solar energy, and mixing species with different rooting patterns can more fully exploit soil resources. Species may also have differing phenologies of root or shoot growth resulting in lower competition between individuals for soil water or nutrients (Lamb and Lawrence 1993).

Planting a mixture of faster growing pioneer species with shade tolerant late-successional species may facilitate the establishment of those rainforest species not adapted to establishing in the microclimate of open situations. Mixtures may reduce insect or diseases, for example planting species from the family Meliaceae together with, or under the canopy of, a companion species can reduce the incidence and severity of attack by the tip moth species (*Hypsipyla* spp.).

There has been extensive debate about whether greater diversity results in ecosystems being more stable and resilient to perturbations that has not yet been fully resolved (Peters 1991). Many exotic plantation monocultures have been relatively free of pests and diseases. Monocultures of native species tend to suffer more problems, and there is likely to be less risk of total failure of the plantation as a result of insect pests or diseases if a mixture of tree species is used.

Inclusion of nitrogen-fixing species has been used extensively in agriculture to improve pasture or crop production, and inclusion of a proportion of leguminous tree species can increase production of non-nitrogen fixers in natural and planted stands on N limited sites (Binkley et al. 1992, Binkley and Ryan 1998). Litter decomposition may also be more rapid, and nutrient availability increased when a mixture of litter from different species is present (Simmonds and Buckley 1990).

Using mixtures can increase the production of merchantable timber by improving the form and bole length of the desired species, although the same result may be achieved with close spacing of light demanding species. Planting mixtures could provide greater economic returns than monocultures. Small logs obtained from thinnings for many rainforest species are usually of low value and including other species in the plantation, such as durable eucalypts that have a higher value for small products like posts or poles, could result in increased value from thinnings and higher overall return from the plantation.

Site protection and nature conservation–A mixture of trees and shrubs can maintain a higher ground cover than a monoculture resulting in greater soil protection which may be an advantage on degraded or eroding sites. A mixture of species is the most appropriate method if the objective is to restore the vegetation of a degraded area to something approximating that of the original forest. Ecosystem restoration attempts to mimic the natural successional pathways and processes that enable ecosystems to recover from major perturbations (Jordan, Gilpin, and Aber 1987). By choosing species with fruit consumed by birds or other frugivores and trees with structures suitable for perching the natural regeneration from seed of other species can be enhanced (Guevara et al. 1986, McClanahan and Wolfe 1993, Goosem and Tucker 1995).

Social and aesthetic benefits–Landscape values are becoming increasingly important in many societies and the aesthetic appearance of forestry practices are coming under increasing scrutiny. Many people object to the visual impact of large scale plantations of exotic monocultures on rural landscapes. Planting a mixture of species increases the heterogeneity and improves the appearance of the plantation. This does not necessarily mean planting an intimate mixture of species in a single stand and could include separate smaller plantings of individual species. In general, mixtures of local species are more consistent with the natural landscape and this is likely to result in broader community support for plantation projects. Planting a mixture of species, including those with economic products other than wood, such as fruit, nuts, or medicines, can result in a wider range of products and benefits for the landowner and the local community in developing and developed countries. Inclusion of alternative products that become available from the plantation more quickly than timber products can improve the economic attractiveness of plantation development for private landowners, and result in a greater amount of reforested land. However, more experience is needed in most cases to develop management systems to produce multiple products.

The major disadvantage of mixtures is that they are more difficult and expensive to manage. For example, species in a mixture may grow at different rates and require different harvesting times. This may lead to the possibility that a slower growing species is damaged when the earlier maturing species is removed. Potential production benefits have not always been realised and both production gains as well as losses have been observed (Burkhart and Tham 1992, Wormald 1992, Kelty 1992).

These difficulties are often due to our lack of knowledge about how species are likely to interact. Identifying appropriate plantation mixtures requires a good understanding of the ecology of individual species and comparison of the long-term growth of mixtures and monocultures in replicated, larger-scale experimental or designed operational plantings across a range of sites, however, there are relatively few such experiments.

In the short-term computer modelling may provide an indication of how different species might behave in mixtures. A model with potential for this analysis was developed to predict growth of native rainforests under silvicultural management in north Queensland (Vanclay 1994). Model parameters for recruitment, growth and mortality were derived from measurements of diameter growth on over 200 permanent plots in native forest, some with a measurement history extending over 40 years.

In a recent study this model was used to compare growth of an important rainforest timber species: *Flindersia brayleyana* (Queensland maple), when grown in monoculture and in mixtures with varying proportions of four native pioneer species: *Omalanthus populifolius*, *Elaeocarpus grandis*, *Alphitonia petriei* and *Acacia aulacocarpa*. The modelled plantation regime was to plant 500 stems/ha and grow the stand for 60 years.

The model predicted that *F. brayleyana* growing alone would achieve a merchantable volume (trees > 40 cm dbh) at age 60 years of 321 m³/ha or a mean annual increment (MAI) in volume of about 5.4 m³/ha/yr (Figure 1). This is similar to growth rates achieved in 55 year old plantations that had received minimal silvicultural management. Indicating that the predicted yield in the mononculture is similar to field measurements. Increasing the proportion of different companion species had significantly different effects. Predicted merchantable volume when *F. brayleyana* was grown with the short-lived *O. populifolius* was almost identical to that predicted when it was grown in the same numbers alone. In contrast, a mixture with only 20% of *A. aulacocarpa* resulted in a substantial decline in final volume of *F. brayleyana*. This is consistent with other studies of *Acacia-Flindersia* mixtures (Keenan, Lamb, and Sexton 1995). Increasing proportions of *Alphitonia* and *Elaeocarpus* resulted in a less rapid decline in volume than *Acacia*.

FIGURE 1. Predicted merchantable volume and average stems size of *Flindersia brayleyana* (Queensland maple) at age 60 years using a native forest growth and yield model developed by Vanclay (1994). The model was indicated with 500 stems per ha with an average DBH of 1 cm. Lines show the effect on yield of replacing *F. brayleyana* with 20, 40, 60, 80 and 100% of four rainforest pioneer species: *Omalanthus populifolius, Elaeocarpus grandis, Alphitonia petriei* and *Acacia aulacocarpa*.

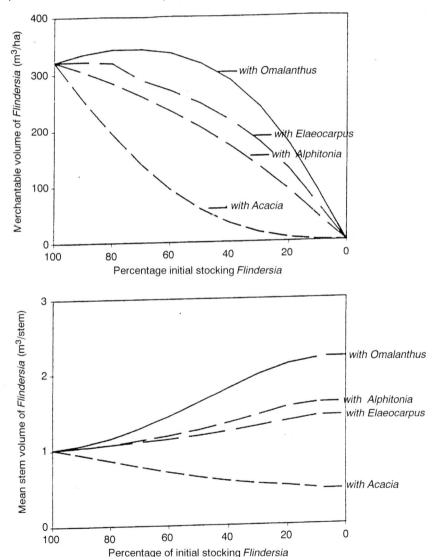

The mix *Elaeocarpus* and *Flindersia* was explored further (Figure 2). Results from this mix indicated that within the range 30 to 70 percent *Elaeocarpus* higher yields could be achieved with the mixture than with either species growing in monoculture.

These results indicate that the growth of target trees in mixtures might vary considerably depending on the nature of the associated species. Species with rapid early growth and dense spreading crowns such as *Acacia aulacocarpa* or *A. mangium* are likely to be unsuited for mixtures with slower growing species. Combining *F. brayleyana* with other species such as *Elaeocarpus grandis* or *Alphitonia petrei* may result in increased production compared with monocultures. While the results are preliminary they indicate that a model based on species behaviour in native forests may be of value in investigating their interactions in plantation mixtures. The model also demonstrates the kind of forest planning tools that will be required to manage more complex plantation designs.

FIGURE 2. Predicted merchantable volume of *Flindersia brayleyana* (Queensland maple) and *Elaeocarpus grandis* (silver quandong) at age 60 years using a native forest growth and yield model developed by Vanclay (1994). The model was initiated with 500 stems per ha with an average of DBH of 1 cm.

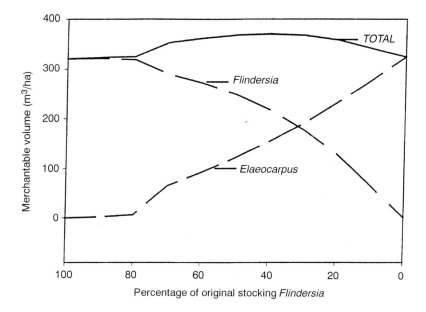

FACILITATING UNDERSTOREY REGENERATION

It has been observed for some time that timber plantations established on degraded sites or grasslands may provide more suitable conditions for regeneration of native plant species that cannot establish in exposed microclimatic conditions or under competition from grasses (Lugo 1992, Parrotta 1993).

This phenomenon was recently investigated at a range of sites across the tropics (Parrotta and Turnbull 1997) including four sites in north Queensland (Keenan et al. 1997). Results from the Queensland study indicated there was considerable natural regeneration under plantations of both native (*Araucaria cunninghamii, Flindersia brayleyana*, and *Toona ciliata*) and exotic (*Pinus caribaea*) species ranging from 5-63 years in age. In total, 350 vascular plant species were found in the plantations. Tree species dominated recruitment (176 species) in both young and older plantations but most life forms were present in most plantations. Older plantations had appreciably more understorey species overall than younger ones and some of this recruitment had grown to become part of the plantation canopy. Diversity of understorey recruitment was higher in plantations of the native species than the exotic and there was a greater diversity of tree species found under the broadleaved species *F. brayleyana* and *T. ciliata*. Most recolonising tree species were primarily dispersed by birds, with wind dispersal of secondary importance, with mammals only responsible for a small proportion of regenerating species.

In general, understorey recolonisation is dependent on the degree of site degradation, proximity to native forest seed sources, characteristics of the planted species, and the age and management intensity of the plantation (Parrotta and Turnbull 1997). The catalytic effect appears to be stronger on wetter than drier sites, perhaps because of there is less competition for moisture and litter accumulation on wetter sites. Adding species diversity and structural complexity generally promotes more rapid and diverse understorey recolonisation, because of the attractiveness of the plantations to a wider variety of seed dispersers. Larger-seeded species are less likely colonise sites due to dispersal limitations, and direct seeding or planting of these species will be required to facilitate their establishment.

STRUCTURING RAINFOREST PLANTATIONS FOR WILDLIFE

Plantation monocultures often support little wildlife (Bevege 1974, Disney and Stokes 1976, Driscoll 1977, Fisher 1974, Heinekamp and Ramsay 1973). Use of plantations by wildlife might be improved by increasing structural and compositional diversity in the ways described above. Bird species diversity is often related to foliage height diversity (Recher 1969) and diversity in crown height can be created in monocultures by having a mixed age distribution or allowing development of an understorey (Curtis 1974, Gepp 1986). However, regional species diversity is largely determined by the abundance of food resources and shelter and the composition and structure of wildlife populations will be strongly linked to the composition and structure of plantations (Clout 1984). High bird diversity in rainforests of the humid tropical lowlands is made up of many rare species that specialise in utilising relatively scarce and scattered resources (Kikkawa and Dwyer 1992). Consequently, maintaining bird diversity depends on maintaining high plant species diversity. The importance of older tree with hollows and other structural features such as dead standing trees and down woody debris for wildlife habitat has also been recognised for some time (Harmon et al. 1986).

In summary, structural and compositional diversity to maintain wildlife populations in plantations can be developed by (1) creating a complex plantation age structure, keeping some older planted trees and maintaining areas of open space; (2) establishing mixed stands, particularly incorporating preferred food trees; and (3) keeping or creating dying and dead wood within plantations.

CONCLUSIONS

Recent studies in tropical plantations indicate that there are a range of ways that plantations can be managed to produce a wider range of ecosystem goods and services at both the landscape and the site level. Some practices, such as retention or restoration of native vegetation in corridors or riparian zones should be incorporated into all plantation developments. The use of native species is worth encouraging more extensively for a range of reasons. Mixed species plantations can provide a range of benefits (including increased production) but these may come at some cost and more extensive analysis and experimentation is required before they are likely to be widely applied. The role of plantations in fostering understorey development is an additional benefit of tropical plantations that has not been widely recognised but one that may be useful for restoration programs and for development of plantations with multiple values.

Some of the ideas we describe are not new, and are currently incorporated into codes of practice and operational activities of forestry companies (Table 1). 'Ecological purists' may consider that the forests resulting from using such techniques may not fully reflect the structure, composition or functioning of natural forests. However, it is

TABLE 1. Results from a survey of corporate environmental and social practices used in 18 large forest corporations with management responsibility totalling 4 million ha of plantations or intensively managed forests (after Bass 1997).

Use of the land prior to management:

Less than 1% was old-growth forest
33% was farmland/secondary forest
66% was grassland or 'degraded' farmland
2-27% of the area under each company was now indigenous forest, usually in an intricate mosaic with plantations

Company environmental practices:

most used reduced-impact machines
most of those using clonal material had strict clonal replacement strategies (every 2-5 years)
most used few and/or 'safe' chemicals
90% employed soil conservation measures
70% designed-in wildlife corridors
70% monitor the spread of exotic species
25% produce non-timber forest products on a commercial basis
25% use only 1 tree species, and 40% only 2 species
10% monitor soil/water quality
chemicals use rates are decreasing; for a tree rotation they are about the same as for a farm crop over just 1 year

Company social practices:

Most companies have some sort of access agreement with local people
80% support subsistence or non-commercial use of forests for public fishing or recreation
60% either run an outgrower scheme or provide extension services to small landowners who grow trees for them
25% produce wild meat, fish, oils, firewood and/or honey on a commercial basis

important to recognise that human impacts and future global change are likely to result in future forest ecosystems that differ compositionally and functionally from those current or past ecosystems. Ultimately, the aim across a considerable part of the tropical forest landscape will be to implement production systems that are flexible in the goods and services that they provide and that are resilient to future change. Achievement of landscape-level and regional conservation goals will depend on integrating production with conservation objectives on a substantial proportion of the forest landscape, and not simply by zoning lands for either conservation reserves, where production of economic goods is prohibited, or intensive production areas, where little attention is paid to other ecosystem values.

LITERATURE CITED

Appanah, S., and G. Weinland. 1993. Planting Quality Timber Trees in Peninsular Malaysia. Forest Research Institute of Malaysia, Kuala Lumpur.

Bass, S. 1997. Not by wood alone: how can wood production be consistent with social and environmental demands. In: Marcus Wallenberg Foundation Symposium Proceedings: 11, edited by Anon. Marcus Wallenberg Foundation, Stockholm, Sweden.

Bevege, D.I. 1974. Pine plantations: farm or forest? In: Proceedings VIIth Triennial Conference, edited by Anon. Institute of Foresters of Australia, Caloundra, Australia.

Binkley, D., K.A. Dunkin, D. DeBell, and M.G. Ryan. 1992. Production and nutrient cycling in mixed plantations of *Eucalyptus* and *Albizia* in Hawaii. Forest Science 38:393-408.

Binkley, D., and M.G. Ryan. 1998. Net primary production and nutrient cycling in replicated stands of *Eucalyptus saligna* and *Albizia falcataria*. Forest Ecology and Management in press.

Brown, A.G., E.K.S. Nambiar, and C. Cossalter. 1997. Plantations for the tropics– their role, extent and nature. In: Management of Soil, Nutrients and Water in Tropical Plantation Forests, edited by E.K.S. Nambiar and A.G. Brown. Australian Centre for International Agricultural Research, Canberra.

Bruenig, E.F. 1996. Conservation and Management of Tropical Rainforests: An Integrated Approach to Sustainability. CAB International, Wallingford, Oxon.

Burkhart, H.E., and A.A. Tham. 1992. Predictions from growth and yield models of the performance of mixed species stands. In: The Ecology of Mixed Species Stands of Trees, edited by M.G.R. Cannell, D.C. Malcolm and P.A. Robertson. Blackwell Scientific, Oxford, UK.

Butterfield, R.P. 1995. Promoting biodiversity: advances in evaluating native species for reforestation. Forest Ecology and Management 75:111-121.

Butterfield, R.P., and R.F. Fisher. 1994. Untapped potential: native species for reforestation. Journal of Forestry 92:37-40.

Clout, M.N. 1984. Improving exotic forests for native birds. New Zealand Forestry 29:193-200.

Curtis, H.S. 1974. Birds and native plants of the Tibrogargan southern pine. In: Proceedings VIIth Triennial Conference, edited by Anon. Institute of Foresters of Australia, Caloundra, Australia.

Disney, H.J., and A. Stokes. 1976. Birds in pine and native forests. Emu 76:133-138.

Driscoll, P.V. 1977. Comparison of bird counts from pine forests and indigenous vegetation. Australian Wildlife Research 4:281-288.

Fisher, W.J. 1974. Conifer plantations-biological deserts? In Proceedings VIIth Triennial Conference, edited by Anon. Institute of Foresters of Australia, Caloundra, Australia.

Forman, R.T.T. 1995. Land Mosaics: The Ecology of Landscapes and Regions. Cambridge University Press, Cambridge, UK.

Gepp, B.C. 1986. Birds in pine forests in South Australia. In The Dynamic Partnership: Birds and Plants in Southern Australia, edited by H.A. Ford and D.C. Paton. Government Printer, Adelaide.

Gerlach, L.P., and D.N. Bengston. 1994. If ecosystem management is the solution, what's the problem? Journal of Forestry 92 (8):18-21.

Gilmore, D.W. 1997. Ecosystem management-a needs driven, resource-use philosophy. Forestry Chronicle 73:560-564.

Goosem, S.P., and N.I.J. Tucker. 1995. Repairing the Rainforest. Theory and Practice of Rainforest Re-Establishment in North Queensland's Wet Tropics. Wet Tropics Management Authority, Cairns.

Guevara, S., S.E. Purata, and E. van der Maarel. 1986. The role of remnant forest trees in tropical secondary succession. Vegetatio 66:77-84.

Hale, P.T., and D. Lamb, eds. 1997. Conservation Outside Nature Reserves. Centre for Conservation Biology, University of Queensland, Brisbane.

Harmon, M.E., J.F. Franklin, F.J. Swanson, P. Sollins, S.V. Gregory, J.D. Lattin, N.H. Anderson, S.P. Cline, N.G. Aumen, J.R. Sedell, G.W. Lienkaemper, K. Jr. Cromack, and K.W. Cummins. 1986. Ecology of coarse woody debris in temperate ecosystems. Advances in Ecological Research 15:133-302.

Heinekamp, H.F., and G.W. Ramsay. 1973. A closer look at birds in exotic forests in New Zealand. Forest and Bird 188:16-18.

Irland, L.C. 1994. Getting from here to there: implementing ecosystem management on the ground. Journal of Forestry 92:12-21.

Jordan, C.F. 1993. Ecology of tropical forests. In: Tropical Forestry Handbook, edited by L. Pancel. Springer-Verlag, Berlin.

Jordan, W.R., M.E. Gilpin, and J.D. Aber. 1987. Restoration Ecology: A Synthetic Approach to Ecological Research. Cambridge University Press, Cambridge.

Kahn, J.R., and J.A. McDonald. 1997. The role of economic factors in tropical deforestation. In: Tropical Forest Remnants: Ecology, Management and Conservation of Fragmented Communities, edited by W. F. Laurance, J. Bierregaard, R.O. and C. Moritz. University of Chicago Press, Chicago.

Keenan, R., D. Lamb, and G. Sexton. 1995. Experience with mixed species rainforest plantations in North Queensland. Commonwealth Forestry Review 74:315-321.

Keenan, R.J., D. Lamb, O. Woldring, A. Irvine, and R. Jensen. 1997. Restoration of plant biodiversity beneath tropical tree plantations in Northern Australia. Forest Ecology and Management 99:117-131.

Kelty, M.J. 1992. Comparative productivity of monocultures and mixed species stands. In: The Ecology and Silviculture of Mixed Species Forests, edited by M.J. Kelty, B.C. Larson and C.D. Oliver. Kluwer Academic, Dordrecht, The Netherlands.

Kelty, M.J., and I.R. Cameron. 1995. Plot designs for the analysis of species interactions in mixed stands. Commonwealth Forestry Review 74 (4):322-332.

Kikkawa, J., and P.D. Dwyer. 1992. Use of scattered resources in rain forest of humid tropical lowlands. Biotropica 24:293-308.

Kimmins, J.P. 1997. Forest Ecology: A Foundation for Sustainable Development. Prentice-Hall, Upper Saddle River, NJ.

Knowles, O.H., and J.A. Parrotta. 1995. Amazonian forest restoration: an innovative system for native species selection based on phenological data and field performance indices. Commonwealth Forestry Review 74:230-243.

Lamb, D., and P. Lawrence. 1993. Mixed species plantations using high value rainforest trees in Australia. In: Restoration of Tropical Forest Ecosystems, edited by H. Lieth and M. Lohmann, Kluwer, Netherlands.

Lindenmeyer, D.B., and H.F. Recher. 1998. Aspects of ecologically sustainable forestry in temperate eucalypt forests-beyond an expanded reserve system. Pacific Conservation Biology 4:4-10.

Lugo, A.E. 1992. Tree plantations for rehabilitating damaged forest lands in the tropics. In: Ecosystem Rehabilitation, edited by M.K. Wali. SPB Academic Publishing, The Hague, The Netherlands.

McClanahan, T.R., and R.W. Wolfe. 1993. Accelerating forest succession in a fragmented landscape: the role of birds and perches. Conservation Biology 7:279-288.

Montagnini, F., E. Gonzalez, C. Porras, and R. Rheingans. 1995. Mixed and pure forest plantations in the humid neotropics: a comparison of early growth, pest damage and establishment costs. Commonwealth Forestry Review 74:306-314.

Parrotta, J.A. 1993. Secondary forest regeneration on degraded tropical lands: the role of plantations as "foster ecosystems." In: Restoration of tropical forest ecosystems, edited by H. Lieth and M. Lohmann, Dordrecht, the Netherlands.

Parrotta, J.A., and J.W. Turnbull. 1997. Catalyzing native forest regeneration on degraded tropical lands. Forest Ecology and Management 99:1-8.

Peters, R.H. 1991. A Critique for Ecology. Cambridge University Press, Cambridge.

Poore, D., P. Burgess, J. Palmer, S. Reitbergen, and T. Synott. 1989. No Timber Without Trees. Earthscan Publications Ltd., London.

Recher, H.F. 1969. Bird species diversity and habitat diversity in Australia and North America. American Naturalist 103:75-80.

Seymour, R.S. and M.L. Hunter, Jr. 1992. New Forestry in Eastern Spruce-Fir Forests: Principles and Applications to Maine. Maine Agric. Exp. Stn. Misc. Publ. 716. 36p.

Simmonds, E., and P. Buckley. 1990. The ground vegetation of underplanted mixtures of trees. In: The Ecology of Mixed Stands of Trees, edited by M.G.R. Cannell, D.C. Malcolm and P.A. Robertson. Blackwell Scientific, Oxford, UK.

Streets, R.J. 1962. Exotic Forest Trees in the British Commonwealth. Clarendon Press, Oxford, UK.

Suckling, G.C., E. Backen, A. Heislers, and F.G. Neumann. 1976. The flora and fauna of radiata pine plantations in north-eastern Victoria. Forests Commission, Victoria, Melbourne.

Swanson, F.J., and J.F. Franklin. 1992. New forestry principles from ecosystem analysis of Pacific Northwest forests. Ecological Applications 2:262-274.

Vanclay, J.K. 1994. Sustainable timber harvesting: simulation studies in the tropical rainforests of north Queensland. Forest Ecology and Management 69:299-320.

Weischet, W., and C.N. Caviedes. 1993. The Persisting Ecological Constraints of Tropical Agriculture. Longman Scientific & Technical, Harlow, UK.

Wiant, H.V. 1995. Ecosystem management: retreat from reality. Forest Farmer 54(5):20-23.

Wormald, T.J. 1992. Mixed and pure forest plantations in the tropics and subtropics. FAO, Rome.

Pacific Spirit–
The Forest Reborn

Patrick Moore

SUMMARY. In recent years, there has been a high-profile battle over the future of the forests of the Pacific Northwest of the United States and Canada. These campaigns have increased public awareness of the value of old-growth coastal rainforest, and greater support for the creation of more protected parks and wilderness. Environmentalists have pressed for, and often achieved, higher standards for forest management. Unfortunately, these campaigns have also spread misinformation and confusion about forests and forestry. This paper gives an alternative view of the ecological arguments used to support a drastic reduction in forest harvesting. Contrary to conventional environmental wisdom I argue, for example, that clearcutting of some forests is beneficial for them and for the human species, rather than harmful. To help understand this I explain how misconceptions arose from popular myths about forest life cycles, deforestation, and endangered species. I believe that much of the environmental movement has gone astray and lost its perspective on the subject of forests. All human activity has an impact on the environment, but forestry is the most sustainable of all the primary industries that provide materials for our civilization. Indeed, wood is one of the few renewable materials we use in large quantities. *[Article copies available for a fee from The Haworth Document Delivery Service: 1-800-342-9678. E-mail address: getinfo@haworthpressinc.com <Website: http://www.haworthpressinc.com>]*

KEYWORDS. Benefits of clearcutting, environmental movement, forest management, misconceptions about forestry, old-growth forest

Patrick Moore is Chair of Sustainable Forestry Committee, 4068 West 32nd Avenue, Vancouver, B.C. V6s 1Z6 Canada.

[Haworth co-indexing entry note]: "Pacific Spirit–The Forest Reborn." Moore, Patrick. Co-published simultaneously in *Journal of Sustainable Forestry* (Food Products Press, an imprint of The Haworth Press, Inc.) Vol. 9, No. 1/2, 1999, pp. 135-155; and: *Contested Issues of Ecosystem Management* (ed: Piermaria Corona, and Boris Zeide) Food Products Press, an imprint of The Haworth Press, Inc., 1999, pp. 135-155. Single or multiple copies of this article are available for a fee from The Haworth Document Delivery Service [1-800-342-9678, 9:00 a.m. - 5:00 p.m. (EST). E-mail address: getinfo@haworthpressinc.com].

My main thesis is that the thrust of much of the environmental movement's policy on forests and forestry is logically inconsistent, and runs counter to their more reasonable positions on biodiversity protection and climate change. I hope to give you a different perspective on these issues than that we've all read and learned about over the past years.

If we look at what came out of the Earth Summit in Rio, and out of the recent Earth Summit Plus 5 in New York, we find that climate change, biodiversity, and forests are without a doubt the top three environmental issues in the world today. Most people have focused on one or the other of these three subjects, yet they are inextricably linked, one with the other. It's these important linkages among the subjects that will lead us to a logically consistent approach to land use, energy use, resource policy, agriculture policy, and forestry policy.

TREES

Consider the image of a single tree. Trees are the individual units–the individual organisms–that make up a forest. We need to remind ourselves that it was about 350 million years ago that plants evolved the ability to grow long wooden stems, and hence became what we call "trees." When they did that, they weren't thinking about our desire to cut them up into two-by-fours. They actually had only one purpose in mind. That was to get the crown of the tree, with its needles or leaves, up above the other plants, where the tree could then monopolize the sun's energy for photosynthesis.

Foresters create clearings in the forest so that the new tree seedlings can be in full sunlight. A tree is basically a plant that wants to be in the sun, and with few exceptions, this is the case. If trees had wanted to grow in the shade, they would have been shrubs instead. They would not have bothered to develop this long wooden stem to get their "heads" up high.

BIODIVERSITY

I believe the most important general ecological fact about forests is that forested ecosystems–not the oceans, not the plains, not the deserts–are home to the majority of all known living species. There's a simple reason for this. The living bodies of the trees create an environment that doesn't exist if trees aren't present. The canopy above is now home to millions of birds and insects, and beneath the canopy, in the interior of the forest, the environment is protected from frost in cold climates, from hot sun in warm climates, and from wind in all climates. In combination with living trees, this creates thousands of new habitats, niches, in which species can evolve. These species could not have existed were it not for the existence of the trees themselves.

When my Grandfather came to the rainforest at Winter Harbour on the north end of Vancouver Island just after the turn of the century, he settled as a logger. And he began in the 1930s to clear-cut everything that can be seen from my house by the sea. It's all grown back since then by natural regeneration. More recently, a 15-year-old clear-cut in the rainforest of northern Vancouver Island, where the moist mild climate creates a vegetation which is thick and lush, grows back quickly. We can't make a desert out of the rainforest just by cutting the trees down.

A common belief is that forestry, by its very nature, results in a loss of biodiversity, a reduction in the number of species on the landscape. That's certainly easy to do. If we cut down a native forest, replace it with a monoculture of exotic trees all planted in rows, and spray pesticides on it to kill the "bugs," we will reduce the biodiversity of that landscape. But sustainable forestry with native tree species and a good understanding of other native species in that forest can result in an increase in biodiversity across many landscapes. This is because we can plan for a finer mosaic of forest age classes and ecosystem types than would normally occur in the absence of human intervention.

One of the reasons for this is that many species of flowering plants in particular just don't grow in the shade. We can't walk into a forest and find fireweed or pearly everlasting growing there, but we will find them in open sunlight. Therefore, a landscape that has all different age classes, including newly cleared areas, young forests, medium forests, and old forests, tends to have a higher biodiversity than a landscape that has a single age class of forest across an entire area.

Inevitably, though, as forests grow back from clearing, whether by fire or by logging, the plants that require sunlight die out. The ones that do well in shade–the same species that were in the original forest–come back in again. This is a cyclical process called "forest ecological succession," in which the composition of species changes through time as a forest grows back from a cleared area to a new closed-canopy forest again.

THE SPIRIT OF THE FOREST

Second-growth, or new forests, are commonly portrayed as not only lacking the biodiversity of mature forests, but also lacking their very beauty–indeed, the spirit of the forest. Now that the evil men have come with their chainsaws and cut the trees, God has left the land, and will never return. All manner of biblical metaphors are brought forward about sacrilege, desecration, rape, pillage, and plunder to describe the cutting of trees. This makes excellent headlines, but, fortunately, there isn't any truth in it. I know this, because I can walk through forests which my Grandfather clear-cut logged in the 1930s. When he logged them, he didn't know the word "biodiversity," because it hadn't been invented yet. And he didn't talk about ecology at the breakfast table, before he went out in the pouring December rain to drag the huge trees that were growing there down to the sea, half the time taking the soil with them. And yet, without any reforestation or any intervention at all, the forest is growing back thickly and quickly. There are ravens and deer and wolves and owls and bears living in that forest today. The spirit of the forest has returned, in 60 short years. The beauty has, too.

MONOCULTURE

Unfortunately, the word "monoculture" has been borrowed from agriculture and applied to forestry as if it meant the same thing, but it usually means something very different. In farming, a monoculture means that we clear away the original ecosystem, usually a forest, pile all the debris into a heap and light it on fire, plow the soil every year, and plant the seeds of an exotic food crop such as corn or wheat. That never happens in the absence of human intervention.

In forestry, a monoculture is a forest which is dominated by a single species of tree. Monocultures occur in nature quite frequently. In my home province of British Columbia, about 30 percent of the original forest would be described as natural monocultures–lodgepole pine,

Douglas-fir, some of the spruces, western hemlock. A natural mono-culture forest is a perfectly full-functioning ecosystem. Shrubs and plants grow below the canopy; nobody weeds them out. Birds and insects and squirrels live in the canopy above; nobody sprays them to kill them. There's nothing unnatural about monoculture forests of this type. And yet, because of the association with wheat fields and farm-ing, it is easy to use the term "monoculture" in a propagandist way.

OLD GROWTH

I've looked into it very carefully and there's no getting around the fact that it takes 500 years for a tree to become 500 years old. That is what we call a "law" of nature. Fortunately, it doesn't take 500 years for the characteristics required by species described as old growth dependent to re-emerge in forests growing back from clearing.

Take, for example, a 90-year-old, second-growth forest on the south end of Vancouver Island. It already has all or most of the characteris-tics needed by old-growth-dependent species. Let's use cavity-nesting birds as a fairly extreme example. These birds need standing dead trees, large enough and rotten enough to allow them to dig a hole and go in to have their babies out of the rain. That doesn't happen automat-ically after a forest is cleared. It takes some time. But it doesn't take 500 years–50-100 years will usually do just fine.

There's another side to this, though. You can't do everything in 100 years. A huge cathedral-top cedar snag was left standing, already dead, when my Grandfather clear-cut the surrounding forest in the early 1940s. When the cedar died, it was about 1,500 years old. It's about 4 meters (14 feet) in diameter. When it falls over, if people leave it alone, it will take about 1,000 years to decay into an unrecognizable form. That's 2,500 years for a tiny cedar seed to germinate on the forest floor and grow into this incredibly complex and beautiful form, and then die and decay–all the while providing habitat for millions of individuals of hundreds of species of insects, birds, and plants.

We can't expect foresters to plan on 2,500-year cycles. Cycles on the order of 250 years are hard enough to think about–never mind what we're going to do next week-end. Therefore, if we want some of the long-term natural cycles to continue across landscapes, there's no real option other than to set aside large areas as protected parks and wilderness. That's why I'm very pleased that in my province of British

Columbia we are now embarked on a process of doubling the amount of land in protected parks and wilderness, and we're doing it on as representative an ecosystem basis as we possibly can.

Long-term cycles cannot coexist over landscapes with intensive forest management, in which we cut trees every 40-100 years. We need to have wilderness set aside if we want the long-term cycles to continue.

ECOLOGY AND AESTHETICS

Most of our Moms taught us not to judge a book by its cover, or, to say it another way, beauty is only skin deep. Nonetheless, we are easily tricked into thinking that, if we like what we see with our eyes, it is good, and, if we don't like what we see with our eyes, it is bad. We tend to link our visual aesthetic to our ethical or moral judgment of things, particularly landscapes.

The Sierra Club helps us make this linkage by saying in their book, *Clearcut: The Tragedy of Industrial Forestry*, "You don't have to be a professional forester to tell if a forest is mismanaged anymore than you have to be a doctor to tell if a person has ill health. If a forest appears to be mismanaged, it is mismanaged." Of course, they're wrong on both counts. You do have to be a doctor in many cases to tell what a person is infected with, and you do have to be a professional forester to tell if a forest is healthy. The Sierra Club says that, because they want us to think that a recently logged area is bad, because it is ugly, wasted looking, and dead. There's no question that it's ugly. But what is it really? It's actually just large lumps of dead wood lying on beautifully fertile forest soil. It's not toxic waste. It isn't nuclear. It's 100 percent organic. And, in fact, many types of forests require site disturbance in order to grow back quickly and healthily. But, we're told, we should judge clear-cuts to be wrong, because they look ugly to our eyes.

Taken in the right light, even clear-cuts can look pretty. Think for a moment, metaphorically, of the clear-cut as a temporary meadow. It's temporary because it's not going to stay this way. It's going to grow back into a forest again. But it's meadowlike for the time being. The trees have been removed, and light can stream in to the ground and foster the growth of plants and other species unable to grow in the shade of the forest.

Meadow and clear-cut used in the same sentence? That's ridiculous. Meadows are beautiful, pleasant places. Clear-cuts are ugly, awful places. Our judgment of meadows and clear-cuts has nothing to do with biodiversity. Meadows are nice places, because they are easy to walk across, sunny, and we can lay our picnic blankets down for a nice time. Clear-cuts are awful places, because we're likely to break a leg within the first 3.05 m (10 ft) of trying to get through the jumbled-up, broken limbs and tops and stumps.

Meadows are actually small deserts. The reason most of them exist is that the site is too dry to support trees. That's why it's easy to walk across meadows. In contrast, clear-cuts are full of trees, because they are wetter environments. Clear-cuts will, in fact, support a far higher amount of biodiversity, a much wider range of species, than will meadows, which can only support drought-tolerant species such as grasses.

Sometimes our eyes tell us the truth about our values. A young Douglas-fir seedling growing in a logged-over area looks beautiful. It is good, because we want it to be there. Sometimes our eyes tell us the truth, and sometimes they lie. That's why we can't trust our eyes, our visual aesthetic, to judge the ecological health of the land.

Fifteen years after clear-cutting, even as the trees begin to come up and dominate the land, the land still "thinks" it's a meadow. The sun still reaches the ground, and fosters the growth of beautiful flowers. As those trees continue to grow up and gradually shade the land, as the trees in older forests have done, all of that beautiful biodiversity will perish in the shade. All of those flowers will die. Would it make sense to go out now, quickly, and snip off those trees with a chainsaw to save the flowers from certain death? Well, no, because we want a new forest to grow there. But you go to some places in this world–Sweden, Germany, Scotland, New Zealand, even Canada–where people are campaigning in the name of conservation to prevent the reforestation of land that was cleared for agriculture centuries ago, because they want to maintain the natural character of the landscape as they have known it since they were born. They don't want a dark spruce forest shading out all the wildflowers on the sheep pasture.

It's important for us to differentiate whether or not the way we think the land should look is based on social, cultural, and personal values as opposed to anything to do with biodiversity or science. There would be nothing wrong with cutting trees down and leaving a piece of land in a meadowlike state. It's perfectly biodiverse and beautiful in its own right. There's also nothing wrong with letting the trees grow back and shade out the flowers, because there are other species that would rather have the trees there. There is no perfect ecosystem for any given piece of land. In fact, there are many different assemblages of biodiversity that are perfectly sustainable on any given piece of land.

SPECIES EXTINCTION

To listen to some groups, particularly my friends in Greenpeace and the World Wildlife Fund, you'd think that species were going extinct by the hundreds every day in the forests of the world. In 1996 in Geneva, the World Wildlife Fund used, as a platform, the first meeting of the Intergovernmental Panel on Forests to make a big press announcement that was carried around the world on AP wire. They said that 50,000 species were now going extinct each year as a result of human activity. Most importantly, they said the main cause of that rate of species extinction is commercial logging. Those are the words they used. Since then, I have challenged them to name a single species that has gone extinct in Canada as a result of forestry activities, where forestry is the main use of the land, and they have not provided me with a single Latin name. They have suggested that the ivory billed woodpecker is a species that went extinct because of forestry in the southeast United States. They haven't been able to name one species for the US Pacific Northwest.

Extensive clearance of land for agriculture in the U.S. Southeast is no doubt the main cause of habitat loss and destruction, and probably the main cause of the ivory billed woodpecker's demise. Forestry may have had a small amount to do with it. But where are the lists of thousands? If 50,000 species a year are going extinct and the main cause is logging, surely we can require that more than one species of bird, which had a questionable relationship with logging, is named.

The spotted owl is one of the species that I do not believe is endangered with extinction because of logging. But in the early 1990s, as you may know, 30,000 people lost their jobs in the US Pacific Northwest as a result of the concern that the northern spotted owl might go extinct if forestry were allowed to continue in the public forests in this part of the world. Since that time, in a short 5 years, a number of things have been discovered. For example, the reassessment of owls on public forests in Washington state has shown, by actual field observation, that there are more than twice as many of these creatures as were thought possible to exist theoretically. It has also now been shown that the belief that spotted owls can grow only in pristine ancient forests is a myth.

Over 350 recorded spotted owls have been found to live on Simpson Timber's redwood forests in northern California, where no old growth, except a few remnant trees, remains. All of these owls are happily mated and breeding in various ages of second-growth redwood. Even though we've gained knowledge that there are far more owls than we thought there were, and that they can live in landscapes that have a large component of second growth, the policy hasn't changed. The public is still told that the owl is threatened with extinction even though logging has been reduced to less than 20% of what it was in the early 1990s.

A species that is truly endangered, one that we don't hear much about, is the Vancouver Island marmot, endemic to Vancouver Island. Only 220 of these animals exist, and only 20 of these are breeding females. This animal is so close to extinction that six of them have been taken out of the wild for a captive breeding program. That way, if the marmot does go extinct, we will be able to do re-introductions. You don't hear people campaigning, in huge fund-raising efforts, to save this species from extinction, yet the spotted owl is on the front page of every newspaper in the nation.

There is a simple reason why forestry generally does not cause extinction. We tend to think that forests need our help to grow back after logging. Of course, they don't. Forests have been recovering from destruction far worse than logging ever since forests began. Ten thousand years ago, 30 percent of the existing forests in the world didn't exist–Russia, 20 percent; Canada, 10 percent. All were covered by a sheet of ice right down to mineral and bedrock, with nothing living there. Yet, when the ice retreated, the forest grew back. The same occurs after fires, volcanoes, floods, landslides, and so forth.

If forests were not capable of recovering from total destruction, they wouldn't have been there in the first place. The corollary to this statement is that every single species in the forest must be capable of recolonizing areas of land that have been devoid of forest as the forest renews itself–or they wouldn't have been there in the first place either.

Forest renewal is the sum total of each of the individual species reoccupying that piece of land, as the land becomes suitable for each of them, in turn. It takes a while for cavity-nesting birds to be able to breed in a new forest, but most of them can feed there very quickly, as berries grow back in the sunshine. This is really why forestry doesn't generally cause the extinction of species. As long as we let the forests grow back, the species will come back into and recolonize those areas.

FIRE

Fire has been the major agent of forest destruction–or disturbance, as ecologists like to call it–since forests began. That's OK, we're told, because fire is natural; it does not destroy the forest ecosystem. Logging is unnatural. Nature never comes in with logging trucks to take the trees away.

But nature does come in and take the trees away. The black smoke that blows downwind when fire goes through a forest is the carbon that came out of the trees. All the ash that remains on the forest floor, and washes into the streams with the first rainfall, contains the minerals that were in the trees. Every day, as litter on the forest floor decomposes, the silt washes into creeks and rivers, and goes downstream to form fertile deltas where we grow most of our good food. Those deltas are made out of the bodies of the trees that were living farther upstream and farther up the hillside. Nature does take the trees away. Every day. And sometimes in a cataclysmic fashion, as with fire. Just not with logging trucks.

If you think fire doesn't destroy the ecosystem, count the species after a hot forest fire. Not only are all living things above the ground killed, but, in very hot fires, the soil is sterilized right down to bedrock or mineral. The seeds are killed, too. So, basically we're left with a sterilized landscape, something that forestry rarely, if ever, accomplishes.

A good example of this can be found in the Grand Prismatic Basin in Yellowstone National Park, where fire burned 404,700 hectares (a million acres) and resulted in the biggest effort–U.S.$125 million–to put out a forest fire in the world's history. Seven years after that fire, there are no young pine trees growing up under the dead ones, because the soil was damaged so badly.

There are some green plants growing there, but not from seeds that were in the soil after the fire–rather from seeds that have blown in subsequently on the wind. Seeds of species such as cottonwood, dandelion, and fireweed, i.e., seeds that will travel for 161 km (100 mile) on light air, will settle out on a place like this, germinate, and begin the process of healing the soil and getting some carbon and organic matter back into it again. But it will be a long time before pine trees grow there again, because there are no seeds around, and pine seeds don't travel 161 km (100 miles) on a light wind. Yet, they may come back quicker than we think. It was Thoreau, in fact, who figured out over 100 years ago, being about 100 years ahead of his time in understanding forest ecological succession, that pine trees hold onto many of their seeds right into the dead of winter, and don't let them go until February. What kind of crazy tree would drop its seeds onto the snow? A tree that "knows" that those seeds will blow across the slick surface of the snow for miles, across frozen lakes and frozen rivers, and disseminate far wider than they ever could if they simply fell on the ground and got stuck there.

Close by, a healthy new pine forest is coming up quickly. Here the soil is wet, because it's a seepage site, and, even though everything aboveground was burned to death, the seeds survived the fires. Up comes a new forest, thicker than the hair on a dog's back.

Fire can be extremely destructive, and result in a tremendous setback in ecological succession. Fire can also be less destructive, and result in a rapid renewal of the forest. And, of course, on many occasions, fire just burns the lower vegetation and doesn't even kill the trees.

Logging is no different in that sense. If we do forestry in a way that damages the soil severely and causes erosion and the like, we will cause a set-back in ecological succession similar to that caused by fire. But, if we do forestry properly, we may have rapid recovery of the forest, and no set-back in the productivity of the site.

INSECTS

In British Columbia insects are the next major cause of forest death after fire. The bark beetle is one insect that is completely uncontrollable, and sometimes, in the period of a few years, will kill thousands of hectares of trees over broad areas of the landscape. We have a choice when this happens. We can do what they did in northern Idaho, where there was a campaign against salvaging timber, and just let the dead trees dry out in the sun. Soon lightning will strike, and the whole thing will go up in a conflagration, damaging soils, killing millions of creatures, and usually taking out adjacent areas of healthy forest. At the end of that process, we have a damaged ecosystem and no money.

We take a different approach in British Columbia. We do what's called "chasing beetles." As a forest is infested with beetles, we quickly change our forest plans. Quite often we can refocus within a period of weeks or months, and start cutting the trees as they die. That way we get some jobs. And we produce some wood. And we get some chips for pulp. And we make some money. We use some of that money to reforest the area cut—quickly. The soil has not been damaged. Not as many creatures have lost their lives. And the surrounding forest is intact. This approach makes more sense to me.

The Sierra Club has a picture of a particular clear-cut in the Matthew River Valley on the western slopes of the Caribou Mountains in British Columbia in the book, *Clearcut: The Tragedy of Industrial Forestry*. The area was logged after beetles killed the trees. The caption for the picture talks about the greed of the multinational forest corporations and the destruction of the temperate forests of North America. The Sierra Club conveniently forgot to mention the beetle.

Beetles refuse to recognize the maximum clear-cut size of 60 hectares in B.C.'s Forest Practices Code. And so we do sometimes end up with rather large openings as a result. It doesn't make much sense to us to leave big strips of dead trees in the middle. But it's not fair to characterize this as forest policy in British Columbia unless the beetle is mentioned. The beetle is the reason we do this, not because we favor 2,000-hectare clear-cuts.

VOLCANOES

Of course, one of the best places to go to see the effects of nature, and the destruction of the forest by nature, is Mount St. Helens in Washington State. When Mount St. Helens blew up in 1980, the mountain took out 60,705 hectare (150,000 acre) of adjacent forest to the north of the cone. Interestingly, that forest was in two main jurisdictions: federal forest, part of the Gifford Pinchot National Forest controlled from Washington, DC, and private forest, owned by Weyerhaeuser. The U.S. government redesignated their part the Mount St. Helens National Volcanic Monument, where "nature would be permitted to recover, uninhibited by human beings, for the study of science." Sixteen years after the volcano erupted, nature, recovering uninhibited by human beings, still looks pretty much like a wasteland. Dead trees lie where they were blown over or had their tops ripped off by the blast, and there is a 0.30-0.61-m (1-2-foot) thick layer of volcanic ash, which makes a very sterile seed bed. Only a bit of slide alder, which is a nitrogen-fixing plant, has been able to come in and establish itself in those number of years.

Weyerhaeuser took a completely different approach. First, they salvaged all the dead timber. Sites on Weyerhaeuser land originally looked just like those on federal land. Eighty-five thousand three-bedroom homes worth of timber was taken off during two hot summers of intensive salvage operations. They had to invent a carbide-tipped chainsaw, because the ash was so abrasive to normal chains they couldn't use them. They had to put a breathing apparatus on all their workers, because of the dust. But they did it.

Almost inadvertently, bringing in the heavy equipment and dragging around the old-growth timber, they disturbed the site so dramatically that it stirred the underlying organic soil to the surface. This classic case of site disturbance, or "site preparation," as it's called when it's done on purpose, created a more fertile and productive area than would have been there with no disturbance. Of course, every farmer knows that plowing the field makes the crops grow better.

Then Weyerhaeuser planted 2-year-old Douglas-fir and noble fir, nice big seedlings, which were able to get their roots established before they died of drought or starvation. In 2024, there'll be a crop of timber off this land, while the national volcanic monument will still be barely recovering.

I'm not making a value judgment about which approach is good or bad. It's interesting to see how nature works, too. But isn't this dramatic evidence that a couple of interventions by human beings can make a really big difference in the way in which an ecosystem recovers after a natural disaster?

NATIVE TREE SPECIES

With all the talk about monoculture pulp plantations and fiber farms, we might easily forget that people in many countries don't even use native tree species for commercial forestry. The classic case is

New Zealand, where almost 100 percent of the forestry is done with exotics, mostly radiata pine from California. What's the matter with the kiwis? Don't they like their own trees?

They do, actually, like their own trees. Their own trees have very good wood qualities. Unfortunately, not a single species of native New Zealand tree grows fast enough to be useful for commercial purposes. They can't wait 150 years for an 20-cm (8-inch) sawlog. That's why 80 percent of New Zealand was deforested before they started their exotic reforestation program. When they cleared forests in New Zealand, it wasn't worthwhile to put new trees on that site, if they were native species. New Zealanders turned these sites into sheep farms, instead. Now they are reforesting 100,000 hectares a year with exotic species, and creating the underpinnings of the economic turnaround in New Zealand. Those new forests aren't very similar to the native forests that once grew there.

In Scotland, people use larch from China, Douglas-fir from Oregon, and spruce from the Queen Charlotte Islands for most of their reforestation. In Sweden, they are using lodgepole pine from British Columbia. They like it a lot. It grows faster than the native Scots pine. And straighter, too. In Brazil, they use *Eucalyptus* from Australia for most of their pulp and paper plantations.

Now I'm not against those things. But surely we should examine, in perspective, what we're doing here, where we do use native tree species, and where more and more we use seed from the same place and try to create the same types of mixtures that were present in the original forests. The point is, managed forests in North America are more similar to the original forests than are those in nearly any other place in the world.

DEFORESTATION

My core message is about deforestation. Deforestation is described by the United Nations as "the permanent removal of the forest and the conversion of the land to another use, such as agriculture or human settlement." But, combined with the aesthetic problem, people are easily convinced that a recent clear-cut is a scene of deforestation. For some reason, our eyes don't like jumbled up, unorganized bits of woody debris lying about on the land. Of course, when the new forest grows back up above the jumble of wood, and provides a constancy of green across the land, it'll look fine to us. But, for now, we're easily convinced that an ugly clear-cut is deforestation.

Most people find farm fields quite pleasant–pastoral and lovely. Yet farm fields are a scene of deforestation. All that land was in native forest before the farms came in. If people were to stop plowing those fields for 5 years, seeds from the surrounding trees would blanket the area with new tree seedlings. Eighty years later we'd never know that a farm had been there.

Deforestation is not an event that just happens, and then is over. Deforestation is an on-going process of interfering with forest recovery, and preventing the forest from coming back. The commonest form of that interference is what we call "agriculture." That's why deforestation is seldom caused by evil corporate overlords in multinational forestry headquarters. Deforestation is nearly always caused by friendly farmers growing our food, and by nice carpenters building our cities and towns.

Remember when McDonald's promised they would never buy another tropical cow because of fears of deforestation in Central and South America? I'm sure the North American cattle industry thought that was a good idea. Do we have a higher caliber of deforestation up here than they do down there? Of course, we don't. A temperate rainforest turned into a cattle farm has lost its native biodiversity in a way no different than that in which a forest in Costa Rica or Brazil loses its biodiversity when it is converted to a cattle ranch. Those who don't eat meat have to have vegetables, and will cause the creation of monoculture cabbage plantations throughout the land. They look nicer than clear-cuts. They're quite pretty, in fact. But where is the biodiversity? All in the surrounding forests.

I'm not against farming, of course. I know that we have to clear part of the forest away in order to grow our food and house our population. But wouldn't it be a good idea if the first principle of biodiversity conservation were to minimize the amount of forest cleared for farms and towns, thus maximizing the amount of land that remains in forest, whether for timber production or protection? We don't do this. Instead, we sprawl our cities and towns across the land, as if it were endless. We usually cover up the best soils in the process, thus making it necessary to go deeper into the native forest to clear it in order to grow our food. We don't do what we should be doing to protect

biodiversity. It has nothing to do with ending logging. It has everything to do with retaining forest cover.

Bales of hay are pleasant looking in the late afternoon light, but
what are they really? Large lumps of dead cellulose, lying on a deforested piece of land. The native biodiversity will be found in a nondescript scrub hardwood in the background vegetation. Monoculture is
often pretty; biodiversity is often nondescript.

A *Zinnia* plantation in Australia is gorgeous, beautiful, and colorful.
Yet it's also a monoculture, requiring pesticides every day. A nearby
gray-green *Eucalyptus* forest has over 20 species of *Eucalyptus* and
other hardwoods, and hundreds of species of shrubs and herbs and
insects and birds. The monoculture is gorgeous; the biodiversity is
gray-green and bland.

LAND USE AND BIODIVERSITY

The automobile is arguably the most destructive technology ever
invented by the human species, in terms of its impact on biodiversity.
This is especially true when we consider the side effects, such as the
black stuff they roll around on asphalt. Why is it legal to take the toxic
waste out of oil refineries, mix it with gravel, and spread it all over the
surface of the Earth so that cars and trucks can roam about freely?
Think about it.

We put crude oil in an oil refinery. We take the propane off the top
to run the taxi fleets, gasoline off next to run the cars, diesel from a
little lower to run the trucks and trains, and bunker sea crude from near
the bottom to run the big ships across the sea. Remaining on the very
bottom is a black gooey crud–that's what we make asphalt from. If this
material were taken to a government-approved landfill, it would be
turned away at the gate. It's hazardous, toxic, and, in fact, carcinogen-
ic. It's illegal to bury it, yet perfectly OK to spread it in a thin layer
over the surface of the planet, killing everything in its path in the
process. There's no EPA guideline for going out to stop trucks from
dumping this material all over the surface of the Earth. If it were taken
into a lab and tested, the rats would all die from a small dose of it.
Funny double standard we have. It's very cozy for the oil industry,
because the more asphalt we lay down, the more gas and diesel we
need for more cars and trucks, and the more cars and trucks we have,

the more pavement we need. It's a cyclical process, but not quite the same as forest ecological succession.

Think of biodiversity on a scale of zero to 100. You'd have to agree with me that asphalt is close to zero. Modern agriculture is maybe 5, 10, we'd be pushing it at 20, in terms of the number of species that were on that landscape before the original forest was taken down. Forestry, the way it's practiced in the Pacific Northwest in particular, is 96, 98, 100-102, if we increase landscape biodiversity through planning. All this argument and political heat over 2 percent, as far as I can see. It's time we took a broader view of land use and the impact of civilization on biodiversity. We've got to take more into account than a snapshot of a clear-cut 5 minutes after the trees are cut down, when in fact that area is going to grow back into a forest again. It's very unlikely that the asphalt parking lot will grow back; it's probably going to stay like that for a long, long time. That's why I'm glad I'm in wood, rather than in oil.

People are often surprised to learn that wood is, in fact, the most renewable of all the materials we use in human civilization. Why is it so renewable? First, and most people also find this hard to believe, wood is 99 percent air and water. Fifty percent from CO_2 in the air, 49 percent H_2O that falls as rain, and only 1 percent mineral that comes from the Earth's crust, which is very thick and not likely to wear out anytime soon.

And then there's sunlight. Apparently we have 5 billion years of that left over. That's why wood is so renewable, and why, when we remove a tree from a forest, we're not removing very much of the soil or the nutrient content. Only 1 percent of the tree is composed of those things. Mostly what we're taking away is air and water.

WOOD AND PAPER

I carry this little wedge of wood around with me to illustrate that every day, every person in the world uses this much wood–1.6 kilograms. All six billion of us. Six billion times 1.6 kilograms are taken every day from the world's forests. Think of this in terms of how much food we eat, and it's clear that we use far more wood than any other single type of crop or organic material. Just because we don't get hungry for wood every 3-4 hours doesn't mean that it isn't absolutely necessary for our daily existence. In fact, I think it's easier to go a day without food than it is to go a day without wood.

Nonetheless, it's a lot of wood. In North America we use four times that much every day per person. A family of four in the United States uses 15 kg (40 lb) of wood every day, 365 days a year. So, you might say, there's the answer: use less wood. And this is where the thrust of the environmental movement comes in.

The Rainforest Action Network has a wood use reduction program to reduce the use of wood in the United States 75 percent by the year 2010. Sounds good. Use less wood, save more forests. Wouldn't that be wonderful? Unfortunately, it sounds good and it sounds logical, when in fact it is not. People are generally surprised to learn that over half of the wood used in the world is not for building things, but for energy–for cooking and heating, mostly in tropical, developing countries. Unfortunately, unregulated fuelwood gathering is a major cause of deforestation in the Tropics. If we were to take wood away from these people, they would die by the hundreds of millions. They depend on wood for their survival. People in these countries make less than $500 per capita per year, and cannot afford to buy energy substitutes. What are the substitutes? They are fossil fuels, so maybe it wouldn't be such a good idea, even if they could afford them. Switching from wood to fossil fuels would only exacerbate greenhouse gas emissions, and increase the amount of CO_2 in the atmosphere.

Thirty-five percent of all the wood used in industrial countries is for construction, solid wood of one sort or another. All the substitutes, and they are steel, cement, plastic, and brick, require a lot more energy to produce. "A lot more energy to produce" translates, almost invariably, into increased greenhouse gas emissions. Industrial countries have had an almost impossible time as it is in stabilizing greenhouse gas emissions. If we were to start fooling around with the 85 percent of the wood we use every year for fuelwood and solid wood construction, we're only going to make that problem worse.

Only 15 percent of wood use in the world is for pulp and paper. According to Greenpeace, when people blow their noses in England, they're blowing away the ancient rainforests of the Pacific Northwest. The Rainforest Action Network's goal of reducing wood use is to save the forests and save the planet. Most of the pulp and paper in the world is made from sawmill residues and from pulp plantations, most of which are established on land that was already cleared. A component of pulp and paper is made from native forests. There's no doubt of that. In northern Canada, for example, in the boreal forests, we're now basing large pulp mills on aspen in native forests. But most of it comes from these other sources.

If we don't make paper out of wood, what are we going to make it out of? There's a major movement, led by David Brower and others in the environmental movement, to substitute fibers other than wood for paper. "Tree-free paper" it's called, or "wood-free pulp." Again, this sounds like a great idea. If we use an alternative fiber, such as hemp or kanaf, we won't have to cut the trees. One small problem: where are we going to grow the hemp and kanaf? We can't grow it on Mars. It has to be grown on the Earth. In particular, it has to be grown where we could be growing trees. Those crops won't grow in places where we can't grow some kind of woody vegetation, especially in this part of the world.

Why would an organization whose main purpose in life is stated as "the protection of biodiversity" advocate massive monoculture plantations of exotic annual farm crops such as hemp to produce paper when we could be growing trees? Everybody knows that birds and squirrels prefer trees to hemp farms. There is no sense to it at all.

The position against using wood to make pulp and paper runs logically inconsistent and contrary to the position of protecting biodiversity. A couple of quotes from David Brower will indicate that this, in fact, is the thrust of the movement's position. First he says, "Now I'm not saying that we should never cut trees; I'm saying that we have probably overdone it. It's about time we did something else." I think he's saying that we should cut fewer trees. The next quote is, "I have nothing against greater forest growth; I have something against planting trees. Growing forests is quite different from planting trees."

I believe that the environmental movement's position on forestry is in fact anti-environmental in the sense that it runs counter to policies that would promote the protection of biodiversity and reduce the amount of greenhouse gas emissions. We cannot pretend that there are not six billion people waking up in the world every day with real needs for material, energy, and food. Those needs have to be satisfied somehow. In my estimation, the best way to satisfy them is not to reduce wood use and the cutting of trees, but to plant more trees, reverse deforestation, and help developing countries create sustainable fuel-wood plantations close to the towns so that women don't have to walk

5 miles every day to collect enough twigs to cook food at night. Essentially, the best way is to increase the world's forest estate, to take some of the land that's been converted to agriculture and put it back into forest again. Densify the urban environment. Intensify food production. Make more land available for trees.

CONCLUSION

We're very fortunate in British Columbia, as you are here in the Pacific Northwest, to have wild native forests growing right by our cities. They are not botanical gardens, which somebody visits with clippers and prunes the shrubs every year. They are native forests of Douglas-fir, cedar, hemlock, birch, alder, maple, cherry, and so forth–all growing beautifully wild as ever. Nobody is interfering. People who come to Pacific Spirit Park, 800 hectares (2,000 acres) of beautiful wild forest right in the heart of Vancouver, would never suspect that in 1914 that very area was clear-cut to feed the sawmills that helped build the city of Vancouver. The men who cut the forest with double-bitted axes and crosscut saws didn't know the words "biodiversity" or "ecology" any more than my Granddad did. They did this and moved on. There was absolutely no reforestation afterwards. All the forest has returned–some in hardwood, some in softwood. All the beauty has come back to the area, as has the spirit and the fertility of the land. All the biodiversity, all the little things–the bugs, the fungi, the liverworts, mosses, and ferns. The only things missing are the large four-legged mammals, like bear, deer, cougar, and wolf. They've been replaced by the two-legged variety of mammals who come for a stroll by the thousands on a sunny Sunday afternoon. This is an urban park. If Pacific Spirit Park were located farther out in the woods, though, it would provide perfectly good habitat for all those large mammals as well. It is what could be called "a forest reborn," reborn from what today is routinely described as "the total and irreversible destruction of the ecosystem." Because it is a park now, in 100 years from now, our great grandchildren will see an old-growth forest there again.

I believe that, given the tremendous increase in knowledge of biodiversity, conservation biology, forest science, protected areas, soils, and nutrition, we can continue to use our forests as a major source of wood and income base for families and communities, and at the same time make sure that those forests provide a home for all of the many species that require them for their survival. It's time that politicians, environmentalists, teachers, and the general public got that balance right, because we must get it right if we are to achieve sustainability in the 21st century.

May the Forest be with you!

Sustainable Environment
Through Calibrated Resource Taxation

Fedor Semevski
Boris Zeide

Governments tax income, property, consumption (sales and value-added taxes), production, or resources in order to obtain revenues for public services and promote social equality. Income is produced largely (though not exclusively) by energy, initiative, and talent of people. As an undesirable by-product of collecting money for public services, income tax discourages these qualities and thus punishes not only the better-offs but the society as a whole. As far as this method undermines the productive capacity, it defeats the purpose of taxation. Although none of the existing taxes was developed to conserve the environment, by discouraging industry, income tax slows down environmental degradation. Taxation focused on consumption and production would benefit the environment even more.

Presently, economics recognizes two principles of taxation (Samuelson and Nordhaus 1989): the benefit principle–people should be taxed in proportion to the benefit they receive from government programs; and the ability-to-pay principle–people should be taxed in proportion to their ability to pay. These principles were sufficient in

Fedor Semevski is Senior Researcher at the Institute of Global Climate and Ecology, Moscow, Russia.

Boris Zeide is Professor of Forestry at the School of Forest Resources, University of Arkansas, Monticello, AR 71656-3468 USA.

[Haworth co-indexing entry note]: "Sustainable Environment Through Calibrated Resource Taxation." Semevski, Fedor, and Boris Zeide. Co-published simultaneously in *Journal of Sustainable Forestry* (Food Products Press, an imprint of The Haworth Press, Inc.) Vol. 9, No. 1/2, 1999, pp. 157-158; and: *Contested Issues of Ecosystem Management* (ed: Piermaria Corona, and Boris Zeide) Food Products Press, an imprint of The Haworth Press, Inc., 1999, pp. 157-158. Single or multiple copies of this article are available for a fee from The Haworth Document Delivery Service [1-800-342-9678, 9:00 a.m. - 5:00 p.m. (EST). E-mail address: getinfo@haworthpressinc.com].

the past when we were not concerned about changing the environment. They address the chief problem our time–environmental degradation–only indirectly, as a by-product of securing government revenue.

What we need is another principle of taxation, the principle that considers both human society and its impact on the environment. This environmental-impact principle intends to tax the primary source of environmental degradation: resource utilization. This principle does not follow from the two classic ones. It is not a consequence of the benefit principle because the original payers will be large landholders comprising a small fraction of the population. Neither the principle is tailored to the ability to pay. The rich people will not be affected directly (indirectly, everyone of us will be involved as both beneficiary and contributor of resource taxation).

Taxing resources, both renewable and nonrenewable, is the most direct and efficient way to conserve the environment. Taxation of resources differs from that of production. A subsistence farmer working several acres using no-till methods would pay much less per bushel of wheat than a commercial farmer tilling thousands of acres. When farmers, chemical companies, and forest landowners will pay taxes in proportion to polluted water and air, soil erosion, and other damages to tangible or intangible utilities, it would become unnecessary to prohibit tilling erodible soil or emitting noxious gases. Proper taxing should make these and other environmentally destructive activities unattractive economically. The Internal Revenue Service would make the Environmental Protection Agency irrelevant.

Because resources are at the base of the pyramid that includes income, consumption, production, the resource taxation will affect all of them so as to improve the quality of our life and the environment at the same time. A macroeconomic model developed by the senior author predicts a 15% increase in the gross national product in response to the resource taxation. Equally valuable is the contribution to social stability that will result from raising standard of living, switching to small-scale farming, minimizing prohibitions and other intrusions on liberty.

REFERENCE

Samuelson, P.A. and W.D. Nordhaus. 1989. Economics. 13th edition. McGraw-Hill, New York.

Index

Abies alba Mill. See Brognaturo
    fir-beech forests (Italy)
Abies nobalis. See Intolerant species,
    trees
Ability-to-pay principle, of taxation,
    157-158
Acacia genus, tropical plantation and,
    as exotic species, 121
Adaptive management approach,
    forest management
    implimentation, 63
Aesthetics, of forests, 107
Age class distributions, trees, 47-48
Agricultural land. *See also* Cropland
    unproductive, 37
Agricultural production
    natural resources needed for, 41
    role of technology in, 41
Agricultural resources, food supply
    and, 36
Agriculture. *See also* Cropland
    biodiversity and, 151
    deforestation and, 149
    food production and, 36
    resources limited, 36
    species extinction and, 142
Air pollution, population growth and,
    39
Alberese stone pine forest (Italy)
    case study, 66
    cultivation in, 66
    description, 67
    edible seed production and, 66,67
    forest management in, 67
    natural regeneration in, 68
    stands of, 68
Annual revenue, impact of
    silvicultural regimes on, 56
Anthropocentrism, outmoded, 13

Apennine Range, tree mixture in, 67
Artificial interventions. *See also*
    Human interventions
    forests and, 62
    inherent risk in, 66
Asian cheetah, of Turkmenistan,
    reintroduction recommended,
    83
Automobile, impact on biodiversity,
    150-151

Bark beetle, forest death and, 145-146
Bats, protected in Turkmenistan, 85
Bear, protected in Turkmenistan, 85
Bearded goat, protected species, of
    Turkmenistan. *See* Heptners
    markhor
Beech, in Brognaturo forests, 67
Beetle, forest death and, 146
Benefit principle, of taxation, 157-158
Biocenoses, dynamics of, 65
Biocentrism. *See* Ecocentrism
Biodiversity. *See also* Genetic
    diversity
    aesthetic values and, 141-142
    automobile's impact on, 150-151
    British Columbia and, 154
    clearcutting and, 154
    conservation of, in Turkmenistan,
    74
    cultural values and, 141-142
    definition, 1
      defied, 8
      problem with definition, 17
    deforestation and, 149
    ecosystems and, 1
    Edward Wilson, proponent, 7-8
    environmental movement and, 136

damage done by, 17-18
diversity, 6
   preserving, 17
   techniques that promote, 6
ecocentrism and, 17
environmental degradation
   avoidance of cause of, 17-18
   treating symptoms of, 17
ethics and, 12-13,23
evolutionary process of, 22,24-25
forest management approach
    related to, 63
forest management practices and,
   107-108
Forest Service definition, 9
goals of, 1,2,5-6
human needs and
   current, 5-6
   future, 5-6
of large geographic areas
   as ecological policy sea change,
    29-30
   preferred, 28-29
locus of management, indefinable,
   8-9
methods unsound, 12
moral imperative for, 30,31-32
moral righteousness and, 13
morals and, 23
natural resource managers and, 21
nature of, 16
object of, maximizing biodiversity
   as, 7
operational meaning of, 33
premises, 1,2
   "old" forestry not sustainable,
    2-3
public policy paradigm for, 32
purpose of, 2-3,12-13
quality of environment, on global
   scale, 5-6
quantifiable aspects of, 46
revolutionary view of, 25
   assertions of, 25-32
scientific basis for, assertion of
   fundamental values, 32

social policy change and, 22-23
   assertions of, 23-24
sustainability and, 2-3
sustainable environment, problem
   of, 17
tropical forests, alternative options,
   120
tropical timber plantations, 117
   conservation benefits, 117
tropics, 119-120
values and, 23
view of traditional forestry, 3
views of, 22
Ecosystem restoration
   methodologies for, 90
   mixed species plantation and, 124
   objective of, 124
   to previous condition, 90
   role of fire in, 94-95
Ecosystems. *See also* Forest
    ecosystems; Longleaf pine
    ecosystems
   altered, social judgment of, 28
   assertions of
    everything is connected, 28-29
    natural preferable to disturbed,
     27-28
    reality of, 25-27
   attributes of, 25-26
   biodiversity and, 1
   boundaries absent in, 1
   complexity of, 12
   concept of, 9-10
   definition, 25-26
    A.G. Tansley and, 9-11
    dissimilar to organism, 11
    misnomer, 12
    problem with definition, 17
   fire-dependent, 89
   forest, perception of, 59-60
   goods and services, plantations
    managed to provide range of,
    129
   implied benchmark for, 27
   management of
    large, 28

gene pools of, 85-86
plant genetic diversity and, 85-86
Turkmenistan. *See also* Kopetdagh
Range
biodiversity conservation in, 74
biodiversity in, 73
conservation of, 86
study of, 86
future of, 86-87
gene pool in, 82
geological history of, 73
Natural Reserves of, 82
naturalists in, 74-76
progress under Russian imperial
rule, 74
Turkmenistan Department of Natural
Resources and Conservation,
commitments of, 87

Understorey entries. *See* Understory
entries
Understorey recolonisation. *See*
Understory regeneration
Understory, fire and, 89
Understory development, plantation
role in, 130
Understory regeneration
facilitating, 128
plantation management to
facilitate, 118
species, 128
tropical forest plantations and, 120
Understory vegetation
diversity, in longleaf pine
ecosystems, 91
ecosystem restoration and, 94-95
Uneven-aged forests, forest
regeneration, model and, 61
United Nations, deforestation and, 148
United States
National Forests, Pacific
Northwest, 45
water resources in, 38
Urial. *See* Wild sheep

US Department of Agriculture, global
food supply reports, 36
US Forest Service. *See also* USDA
Forest Service
current practices
harvest and, 52
negative cash flow and, 52
U.S. Forest Service, National Forests
divisions, 47
US Pacific Northwest, logging,
spotted owl and, 142-143
USDA Forest Service. *See also* Forest
Service
Chief Dale Robertson, 2-3
Chief Jack Ward Thomas, 2-3
ecosystem management and, 22
ecosystem management and, 2

Vancouver Island marmot
captive breeding program for, 143
endangered species, 143
Vavilov, N.I., Turkmen Experimental
Station of Plant Genetic
Resources, 85
Vegetation. *See also* Flora
retention of natural, forest
plantation and, 121
Volcanoes, Mount St. Helens, forest
destruction and, 146-147

Walnut forests, of Southwest
Kopetdagh, 80-81
Walnut riparian forest, plant species
in, Kopetdagh Range, 80
Water
agricultural consumption, 37-38
resource for crops, 37-38
resource in food production, 37-38
shrinking ground water resources,
41
Water availability, wild sheep and, 84
Water quality
forest management practices, 107
riparian zone and, 121